Excel

ADVANCED SKILLS

ENGLISH

YEAR 5

AGES 10–11

ADVANCED ENGLISH

Get the Results You Want!

PASCAL PRESS

Donna Gibbs

Contents

Introduction

The aim of the ***Excel*** **Advanced Skills: Advanced English** series is to build on and extend students' skills in English. Each book in the series supports the requirements of the Australian Curriculum (English) at each year level.

The series consists of six books, one for each year level, from Year 1 to Year 6. The series is supported by other books in the ***Excel*** **Advanced Skills English** range.

Structure of the book

Each book in the series contains:

- thirty carefully graded, three-page units of teaching and learning activities.
  - Unit A includes a sample informative, imaginative or persuasive text and deals with **Reading and comprehension skills**.
  - Unit B deals with the Conventions of language: **Spelling**, **Vocabulary**, **Grammar** and **Punctuation**.
  - Unit C deals with **Texts in context**. It provides for a deeper analysis and evaluation of the language choices authors make and the ways that readers make meaning from texts.
- four NAPLAN-style tests.
- answers for all questions.

How to use this book

- Students should complete one unit per week. A suggested plan would be to complete the week's Unit A and B page on one day and the Unit C page on another day of the same week.
- After successfully completing a set of units (e.g. 1–7, 8–15, 16–23, 24–30), students should undertake the corresponding NAPLAN-style test.

How to use this book with the *Excel* Advanced Skills: Advanced Mathematics series

For a complete **weekly English and Mathematics program**, use this book in conjunction with the ***Excel*** **Advanced Skills: Year 5 Advanced Mathematics** book. This way a student will have work set for four days a week: two days for English and two days for Mathematics.

How to assess students' progress

- Templates are included in each book of the series that outline the knowledge and skills targeted by the questions in that book. (Please see page 6.)
- The questions move through the subtopics of English in exactly the same order in each book but as there are more questions and more complex material included in later years of the Year 1 to Year 6 continuum, the question numbers vary across the books.
- The results of the work undertaken in Units A and B can be recorded on the marking grid. See ways to use the marking grid on page 4.

Excel Advanced Skills titles

If students are having difficulty in any area, further support is available in other ***Excel*** workbooks. Please see the comprehensive list on page 5.

The *Excel* step-by-step improvement plan

Step 1

Read the introduction on page 3.

Step 2

Read the text below, along with the further explanation about the question templates and marking grids, on pages 6 and 7.

Question templates

These outline the knowledge and skills targeted by the questions in the book. Remember that the questions move through the subtopics of English in exactly the same order.

Marking grids

The results of the work undertaken in Units A and B can be recorded on the marking grid. This is an easy-to-use diagnostic tool that indicates each student's strengths and weaknesses in relation to specific areas of English.

These results can be used to gather extra information about each student's progress and revision needs. For example, see the sample marking grid for Reading and comprehension in the right-hand column:

- When marking answers on the grid, simply mark incorrect answers with 'X' in the appropriate box. This will result in a graphical representation of areas needing further work. An example for the first five units is shown above. If a question has several parts, it should be counted wrong if one or more mistakes are made.
- Remember that you can identify exactly what type of questions a student is having difficulty with in a topic. For example, in the grid above the student is having difficulty with Reading and comprehension evaluative questions.
- There is no marking grid for Unit C.

Marking grid

Reading and comprehension	Literal	Literal	Inferring	Inferring	Evaluative	Evaluative
Question	1	2	3	4	5	6
Unit 1						
Unit 2						X
Unit 3						
Unit 4						X
Unit 5						X
Unit 6						
Unit 7						
Unit 8						
Unit 9						
Unit 10						

This grid indicates that the student needs extra help and practice in evaluative questions.

Step 3

Refer to page 5: ***Excel* books to help you *get the results you want*!**

- Under each topic there is a list of books in our range to help students. Each ***Excel*** book has a comprehensive contents page that will help you find the appropriate pages in the book to target the specific topic you want in each subject area.

Excel books to help you *get the results you want!*

Reading and comprehension

Excel Advanced Skills

9781741254549

Excel NAPLAN*-style Tests

9781741253641

Excel NAPLAN*-style Tests

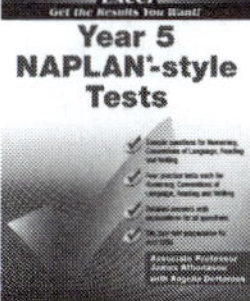

9781741253870

Spelling

Excel Advanced Skills

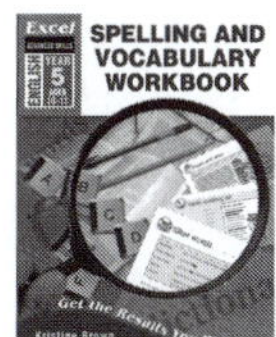

9781741252651

Excel Handbooks & Guides

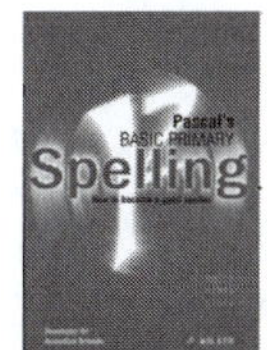

9781864410617

9781741252637

Excel NAPLAN*-style Tests

9781741253641

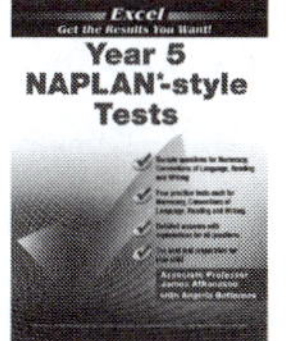

9781741253870

Vocabulary

Excel Advanced Skills

9781741252651

Excel NAPLAN*-style Tests

9781741253641

Excel NAPLAN*-style Tests

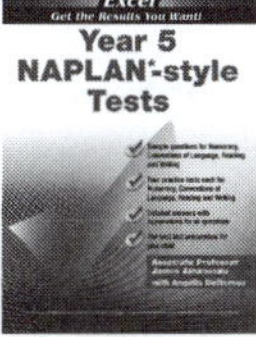

9781741253870

Grammar

Excel Advanced Skills

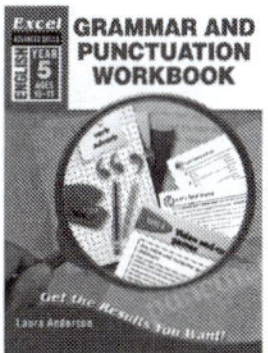

9781741254013

Excel Handbooks & Guides

9781864410600

Excel NAPLAN*-style Tests

9781741253641

Excel NAPLAN*-style Tests

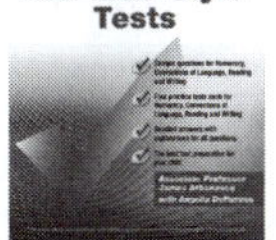

9781741253870

Punctuation

Excel Advanced Skills

9781741254013

Excel NAPLAN*-style Tests

9781741253641

Excel NAPLAN*-style Tests

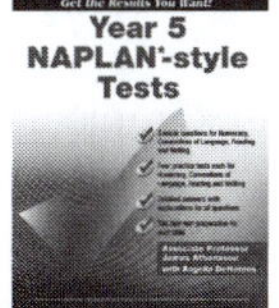

9781741253870

Writing

Excel Advanced Skills

9781741254051

Excel Basic Skills

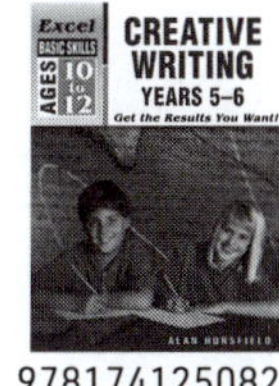

9781741250824

Excel Handbooks and Guides

9781741252835

Excel NAPLAN*-style Tests

9781741253641

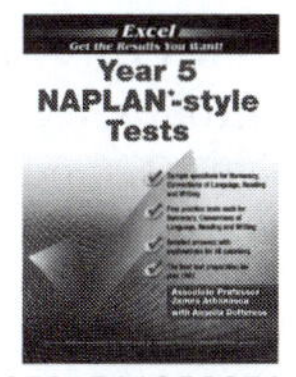

9781741253870

Question templates

Reading and comprehension

Q1–2 Literal: Answers to these questions are found directly in the text.

Q3–4 Inferring: Answers to these questions need to be worked out from clues in the text.

Q5–6 Evaluative: Answers to these questions rely on making judgements about information in the text and beyond the text.

Spelling

Q1–4 Misspelt words: In these questions, students use their understanding of spelling patterns and rules to correct the mistakes.

Q5 Word families: In this question, students use their understanding of base words, morphemes, prefixes, suffixes and etymology to create word families.

Vocabulary

Q6–7 Synonyms: In these questions, students need to comprehend the meanings of words in context.

Q8–9 Definitions: In these questions, students are required to demonstrate understanding of word meanings and usage in the context of the text.

Q10–11 Antonyms: In these questions, students need to understand similarities and differences of meanings.

Grammar

Q12 Nouns/Noun groups: This question deals with subjective adjectives and noun groups that include adjectival phrases and clauses.

Q13 Verbs/Verb groups: This question deals with aspects of verb groups, e.g. subject–verb agreement, modality, auxiliaries and tense.

Q14 Adverbials: This question deals with adverbials, e.g. verb groups that tell when, where and how; modal adverbs; and adverbial clauses.

Q15 Cohesion: This question deals with words that stand for other words, e.g. relative pronouns; and temporal, causal and conditional connectives.

Punctuation

Q16–18 These questions deal with ways of punctuating sentences, e.g. adding capital letters, full stops, question marks, exclamation marks, commas, quotation marks and apostrophes.

Texts in context

Note: There is no marking grid for Unit C questions.

Q1–6 These questions deal with aspects of text, including:

Purpose and audience: These questions require students to recognise the purpose of a text (such as to inform, persuade or entertain) and the nature of its intended audience (the reader, listener or viewer).

Text structures and features: These questions require students to examine how a text is organised to achieve its purpose through, for example, sequencing, paragraphing, and comparing and contrasting.

Textual interpretations: These questions help students to analyse and compare texts and evaluate their effectiveness through, for example, language choices, imagery and point of view.

Get creative

Q7 These tasks require students to create their own texts by adding to or responding to the models provided. Student responses will vary as these tasks are open-ended.

This icon indicates where students will need to use their own paper to answer the question.

Marking grid

Reading and comprehension	Literal	Literal	Inferring	Inferring	Evaluative	Evaluative
Question	1	2	3	4	5	6
Unit 1						
Unit 2						
Unit 3						
Unit 4						
Unit 5						
Unit 6						
Unit 7						
Unit 8						
Unit 9						
Unit 10						
Unit 11						
Unit 12						
Unit 13						
Unit 14						
Unit 15						
Unit 16						
Unit 17						
Unit 18						
Unit 19						
Unit 20						
Unit 21						
Unit 22						
Unit 23						
Unit 24						
Unit 25						
Unit 26						
Unit 27						
Unit 28						
Unit 29						
Unit 30						
Question	1	2	3	4	5	6

Marking grid

Conventions of language	Spelling					Vocabulary						Grammar				Punctuation		
	Misspelt words	Misspelt words	Misspelt words	Misspelt words	Word families	Synonyms	Synonyms	Definitions	Definitions	Antonyms	Antonyms	Nouns / Noun groups	Verbs / Verb groups	Adverbials	Cohesion	Punctuation	Punctuation	Punctuation
Question	1	2	3	4	5	6	7	8	9	10	11	12	13	14	15	16	17	18
Unit 1																		
Unit 2																		
Unit 3																		
Unit 4																		
Unit 5																		
Unit 6																		
Unit 7																		
Unit 8																		
Unit 9																		
Unit 10																		
Unit 11																		
Unit 12																		
Unit 13																		
Unit 14																		
Unit 15																		
Unit 16																		
Unit 17																		
Unit 18																		
Unit 19																		
Unit 20																		
Unit 21																		
Unit 22																		
Unit 23																		
Unit 24																		
Unit 25																		
Unit 26																		
Unit 27																		
Unit 28																		
Unit 29																		
Unit 30																		
Question	1	2	3	4	5	6	7	8	9	10	11	12	13	14	15	16	17	18

READING AND COMPREHENSION

Text 1

Danny's dog

'But why can't I have a dog, Mum?' asked Danny.

'How many times have I explained, Danny? It's not possible because we are out at work all day and you are at school. A dog would be isolated here. It would be lonely and unhappy. It would bark and annoy the neighbours. Dogs are expensive and we can't afford all the expenses involved. Need I go on?'

'But Mum, can't we change things so it would be possible? They might let me tie my dog up in the schoolyard during the day. I could get a paper run and help pay for looking after the dog.'

That sounded very grown-up, Danny thought. Surely now his mum would change her mind.

'Good try, Danny, but the answer is still no.'

***

'Let's play in the garden now, Barney,' Danny said as he patted his imaginary dog.

'Woof, woof.'

'Look there's Ms Parkes's Persian in her apple tree, next door. Barney, stop! Don't chase the cat. Now you've frightened her away. Come back here.'

'Dinner's ready, Danny,' Mum called from the verandah.

'OK, Mum. Just settling Barney.'

'Settling who? I can't see anyone with you.'

'That's because Barney's in his kennel now,' answered Danny. 'Are we having dinner with bones in it tonight?'

'Wash your hands, Danny,' said his mum, shaking her head in despair. Would her son never relent?

1. What does Danny want?
   - A a paper run
   - B to be more grown up
   - C a dog
   - D a kennel for his dog
2. Who lives next door?
   - A a person from Persia
   - B Ms Parkes
   - C Barney
   - D Danny's dog
3. Who or what is Ms Parkes's Persian?
   - A a friend
   - B a rug
   - C a dog
   - D a cat
4. Who says 'Woof, woof'?
   - A Danny's mum
   - B Danny's dog
   - C Danny pretending to be a dog
   - D Ms Parkes
5. Mum's attitude to Danny's behaviour is
   - A patient but frustrated.
   - B impatient and annoyed.
   - C angry and unreasonable.
   - D worried and anxious.
6. Was Mum being reasonable when she refused Danny a dog? Explain.

....

....

....

....

Answers and explanations on page 110

SPELLING

Write the correct spelling of the underlined words in questions 1–4.

1 I don't think that will be posible.

2 I shook my head in dispear.

3 That amount won't cover all the eckspenses.

4 The dog was fritened of the cat!

5 Write three words from the word family that includes **possible**.

VOCABULARY

Circle the answers that have the nearest meaning to the underlined words in questions 6–7.

6 The animal was kept isolated from other animals.
A lonely
B apart
C friendless
D solitary

7 He refused to relent.
A give up
B agree
C relax
D die down

8 Add a word from the text to the sentence.
What .... are involved in looking after a dog?

9 Write a word from the text to match the meaning.
absence of hope ....

Circle the word that does **not** belong.

10 A charges
B costs
C expenses
D money

11 A immature
B grown-up
C adult
D mature

GRAMMAR

12 Add a subjective adjective to the noun group.
My dog has a .... kennel.
A hand-built
B beautiful
C wooden
D brown

13 Add a modal verb (e.g. must, will, can, should, could, might) to the verb group.
'............ I ever be allowed to have a dog?' cried Danny.

14 Complete the sentence with an adverbial from the text that tells **when**.
He hoped to leave his dog at his gran's ....

15 Circle the relative pronoun in the sentence and underline the noun group to which it refers.
Barney was in a kennel that was lined with a soft blanket.

PUNCTUATION

Rewrite the sentences correctly.

16 why wont you let me have a dog mum asked danny

17 ive already explained danny replied mum

18 wash your hands danny said his dad

Answers and explanations on page 110

TEXTS IN CONTEXT

Text 2

Trendhurst Times: LOST and FOUND

Reward offered. I've lost my precious Persian cat, Petunia. She was last seen leaping from my apple tree and speeding away looking terrified though I couldn't see anything chasing her. She will only eat the special cat food I make for her from minced chicken. She likes soy milk. She will be very distressed without me.
If you see her ANYWHERE please phone 0400 444666. Or she can be returned directly to me, Ms Patty Parkes, at 2a Pretty Drive, Trendhurst.

1 What is the purpose of Text 2?
- **A** to tell what happened to Petunia
- **B** to advertise the loss of Petunia so she will be returned
- **C** to describe how it felt to lose Petunia
- **D** to explain why Petunia needs her owner

2 What is the purpose of Text 1 in Unit 1A?
- **A** to tell a story
- **B** to give an explanation
- **C** to recount events
- **D** to discuss a problem

3 In what ways are Text 1 in Unit 1A and Text 2 connected?
- **A** They are both narratives.
- **B** They have a similar purpose.
- **C** They share some of the same characters and events.
- **D** They are both about animal welfare.

4 The tone of Ms Parkes's lost notice is
- **A** calm.
- **B** overemotional.
- **C** pompous.
- **D** thoughtful.

5 Why is the picture in Text 2 important?
- **A** You can recognise Ms Parkes's house.
- **B** It shows the apple tree.
- **C** You can see Petunia.
- **D** You can see the relationship between Ms Parkes and Petunia.

6 What does the picture contribute to the meaning of Text 1 in Unit 1A?

....

....

....

....

....

Get creative

7 Imagine you have lost a pet. Compose an effective 'Lost' notice for your local newspaper.

Answers and explanations on page 110

READING AND COMPREHENSION

 Text 1

Puffin patrols

Announcer: And now for our world news round up. Over 5000 young puffins have been saved from harm this year by the children of Heimaey, a large inhabited island in Iceland. Each year the children carry out the tradition of forming *pysja* patrols (*pysja* is Icelandic for young puffins) to help find lost birds.

Did you know around 60% of the world's puffins live in Iceland? Heimaey is home to many of these much-loved seabirds. At between three and five, when the birds are old enough to breed, they fly back to their birthplace high on the clifftops. There they mate and prepare a nest for their young. The male puffins use their bills to burrow about a metre deep into the soil of the cliffside and their feet to shovel away the loose material. At the end of these tunnel-like structures, they make a safe nest where the females lay a single egg. About six weeks later, the chicks hatch. When they grow stronger, they leave their homes and fly out to sea.

Unsurprisingly, many of these young puffins don't immediately find their way to the sea. Many fly towards the lights of the town and find themselves lost and in danger. This is when the children of the island come to their rescue. In the evenings, they organise patrols to collect lost birds. They keep them safe overnight and then in daylight throw them off the cliffs into the wind, encouraging them to take wing towards the open ocean.

Saving more than 5000 birds this year is a new record. Well done to the children of Heimaey!

1 Heimaey is
- A a type of puffin.
- B an island in Iceland.
- C a resident of Iceland.
- D a tunnel-like structure.

2 *Pysja* patrols are groups of
- A children who collect lost puffins.
- B coastguards in Iceland.
- C baby puffins looking for their mothers.
- D puffin eggs that need looking after.

3 Puffins spend most of their lives
- A laying eggs.
- B at sea.
- C on land.
- D on clifftops.

4 Why do some puffins become disoriented when first heading out to sea?
- A They have poor eyesight.
- B They have poor hearing.
- C They are unfamiliar with the world outside their dark burrows.
- D They are easily distracted.

5 Why do the children throw the puffins off the cliffs?
- A They have finished looking after them.
- B They want them to fly towards the ocean.
- C They are playing a game.
- D They are testing if they can fly.

6 What dangers would puffins face in the town?

....

....

....

....

....

....

Answers and explanations on page 110

SPELLING

Write the correct spelling of the underlined words in questions 1–4.

1 Children enjoy the tredition of *pysja* patrols. ....

2 Some young puffins become lost imediately. ....

3 I wish I could help colect lost birds. ....

4 The girl was encurraging the puffin to fly away. ....

5 Write three words from the word family that includes **organise**.

....

....

VOCABULARY

Circle the answers that have the nearest meaning to the underlined words in questions 6–7.

6 The island was inhabited by Icelandic people.
- A rented
- B tenanted
- C lived in
- D explored

7 Puffins like to burrow deep into the cliffside.
- A drive
- B sink
- C tunnel
- D hide

8 Add a word from the text to the sentence.

Not all the young birds take .... in the right direction.

9 Write a word from the text to match the meaning.

a long-established way of doing something

....

Circle the word that does **not** belong.

10
- A comfort
- B save
- C rescue
- D aid

11
- A harm
- B misfortune
- C hurt
- D blessing

GRAMMAR

12 Add a subjective adjective to the noun group.

The baby puffin was found hiding under a .... car.
- A red
- B parked
- C smart-looking
- D new-model

13 Add a modal verb (e.g. must, will, can, should, could, might) to the verb group.

The puffins .... return to the cliff tops to nest.

14 Complete the sentence with an adverbial from the text that tells **when**.

The eggs are laid and the chicks hatch ....

15 Circle the relative pronoun in the sentence and underline the noun group to which it refers.

The puffin was rescued by a child who was on *pysja* patrol.

PUNCTUATION

Rewrite the sentences correctly.

16 the children saved over 5000 puffins

....

....

17 heimaey is an island in iceland

....

....

18 fortunately the *pysja* patrols save many lives

....

....

Answers and explanations on page 110

TEXTS IN CONTEXT

Text 2

Why visit Iceland?

Iceland is where you can be sure of many once-in-a-lifetime experiences. You can see the northern lights: elusive, green, dancing lights in the sky that will make you believe in magic! You can swim in the crystal blue geothermal springs of the Blue Lagoon; see the Eyjafjallajökull volcano and visit nearby black lava beaches; go ice-climbing; and see their oh-so-appealing, sure-footed, shaggy-haired Icelandic horses.

Call or email for your travel package from *Traveltrue* today.

1 The purpose of Text 2 is to
- **A** inform people about Iceland.
- **B** persuade people to buy a travel package.
- **C** describe some lifetime experiences.
- **D** appeal to the senses of its readers.

2 Where would Text 2 be published?
- **A** in an encyclopedia
- **B** in Wikipedia
- **C** in a magazine or newspaper
- **D** in a geography textbook

3 Text 2 is written to appeal to
- **A** young children.
- **B** adventurous, active holiday-makers.
- **C** lazy holiday-makers.
- **D** people who like art and architecture.

4 The attitude of the author to the subject of Text 1 in Unit 2A is
- **A** matter of fact and low key.
- **B** critical and curious.
- **C** anxious and concerned.
- **D** admiring and congratulatory.

5 Which statement or statements are true?
- **A** Texts 1 and 2 have the same theme.
- **B** Text 1 is spoken and Text 2 is written.
- **C** Text 1 is written and Text 2 is spoken.
- **D** Texts 1 and 2 have different purposes.

6 Does either text make you keen to visit Iceland? Give reasons for your opinion.

....

....

....

....

7 Find out three facts about Iceland that are not included in Text 1 (Unit 2A) or Text 2.

Answers and explanations on page 111

READING AND COMPREHENSION

Text 1

How to make a papier-mâché mask

You will need:

- a balloon
- newspaper torn into strips
- plain paper torn into strips
- papier-mâché glue (Make this from half a cup of flour and half a cup of water stirred together to a smooth paste.)
- scissors and hole puncher
- two lengths of ribbon for tying the mask behind your head
- paint and/or coloured markers.

Method

1. Blow up the balloon until it's approximately the size of your head.
2. Soak the newspaper strips in the glue and coat the balloon. Repeat three times. Let dry completely.
3. Repeat Step 2 using plain paper rather than newspaper.
4. Pop the balloon.
5. Cut the mask to the shape you want.
6. Draw eye-shaped holes and cut out.
7. Punch small holes in the middle of each side of the mask.
8. Thread a length of ribbon through each hole and knot.
9. Paint the mask in a design of your choice.

At last your mask is ready to wear!

1 What size do you make the balloon?
- A the size of a mask
- B the size of your head
- C the size of your ribbon
- D a size of your choice

2 What are the ribbons used for?
- A to decorate the mask
- B to block the holes
- C to tie the mask to your head
- D to put in the holes

3 Why does the paste need to be stirred until smooth?
- A to keep the layers sitting flat
- B to change the mask's appearance
- C to make the mask bulkier
- D to make the paste edible

4 Why do you knot the ribbons?
- A to make the mask look decorative
- B to practise your knotting skills
- C to tie the ribbons together
- D to stop the ribbons slipping through the holes

5 The instructions are
- A confusing.
- B clear and detailed.
- C too difficult for upper-primary students.
- D overcomplicated.

6 What attitude does the author have towards the subject?

....

....

Answers and explanations on page 111

SPELLING

Write the correct spelling of the underlined words in questions 1–4.

1 I stirred the paste until it was very smoothe.

2 You thred the ribbons through the holes.

3 I need the scissers to cut the eye holes.

4 What desine did you choose?

5 Write three words from the word family that includes **blown**.

VOCABULARY

Circle the answers that have the nearest meaning to the underlined words in questions 6–7.

6 The balloon was approximately the size of my head.
A almost B completely
C roughly D less than

7 You need to soak the strips in the glue.
A immerse B put
C drench D drown

8 Add a word from the text to the sentence.
The paper must be .... dry.

9 Write a word from the text to match the meaning.
a decorative pattern ....

Circle the word that does **not** belong.

10 A approximately B exactly
C precisely D definitely

11 A ready B completed
C waiting D unfinished

GRAMMAR

12 Add a subjective adjective to the noun group.
I have made a .... mask.
A papier-mâché
B splendid
C cardboard
D silver

13 Add a modal verb (e.g. must, will, can, should, could, might) to the verb group.
The mask .... not be ready to wear until it has dried thoroughly.

14 Complete the sentence with an adverbial from the text that tells **when**.
.... your mask is ready to wear to the ball!

15 Circle the relative pronoun in the sentence and underline the noun group to which it refers.
Her mask, which was brightly coloured, looked magnificent.

PUNCTUATION

Rewrite the sentences correctly.

16 we used paint and or coloured markers

17 the next step is to blow up the balloon

18 at long last the mask was ready to wear

Answers and explanations on page 111

TEXTS IN CONTEXT

 Text 2

Papier-mâché

The Chinese invented the practice of using papier-mâché almost two thousand years ago. During the Han Dynasty, soldiers' helmets were made using lacquer rather than paste. Japan, for example, developed its own distinctive style of making masks for use in theatre performances and at festivals. In the late 17th century, the French began making and decorating papier-mâché pottery, boxes, trays, and so on. Papier-mâché means 'chewed paper' in French!

1 What is the purpose of Text 2?
- A to inform
- B to persuade
- C to explain
- D to discuss

2 What is the purpose of Text 1 in Unit 3A?
- A to inform
- B to persuade
- C to explain
- D to discuss

3 Text 1 in Unit 3A is aimed at
- A a scientific audience.
- B a general audience.
- C parents.
- D school children.

4 The order in which to follow instructions in Text 1 in Unit 3A is conveyed through
- A time-sequence words.
- B logical connections.
- C sets of connectives.
- D actions listed numerically.

5 Text 1 in Unit 3A is .... Text 2.
- A similar in structure to
- B similar in vocabulary to
- C more formal in style than
- D more informal in style than

6 Do either of the images need captions? Give reasons for your opinion.

....

....

....

....

....

....

Get creative

7 Use the internet to find out what other objects you can make from papier-mâché.

Answers and explanations on page 111

READING AND COMPREHENSION

Text 1

Mary Wade: convict

Mary Wade was born on 5 October 1777. She grew up in a large family in Southwark, an old part of London that fronted the Thames. As a young child, begging became second nature to her and she was found stealing although charges were dismissed. The second time she was caught she was not so lucky. On 14 January 1789, when she was 11, she and a 14-year-old girl, Jane Whiting, were tried at the Old Bailey on a charge of highway robbery.

The charge was that Mary and Jane had tricked an eight-year-old girl, Mary Phillips, into a dark lane where they took off her frock, cap and tippet, leaving her in only her petticoats. They pawned the clothes at a shop for 18 p. The judge accepted evidence from Mary Phillips that the girls had not hurt her. Nevertheless he sentenced them both to death as an example to others. Their sentence was later changed to transportation.

Mary and Jane sailed on the *Lady Juliana*, a ship carrying female convicts, to Sydney on 3 June 1790. Mary was sent on to Norfolk Island on the *Surprise*, arriving on 7 August 1790, and settled there for a time. After returning to Sydney she lived with Teague Harrigan in a tent on the banks of the Tank Stream and had a son, Edward. Teague left on a whaling expedition and didn't return. She is known to have had several more partners and many more children.

When she died on 17 December 1859, aged 82, she is thought to have had around 300 living descendants in her family tree. For this reason, some have named her as a founding mother of early settlers of Australia, a name she probably never dreamed of earning.

1 When was Mary tried for highway robbery?
- A 1777
- B 1789
- C 1790
- D 1859

2 Where was Mary tried?
- A in Southwark
- B on the Thames
- C at the Old Bailey
- D on Norfolk Island

3 Why did Mary beg when she was a young child?
- A She was from a large family.
- B Her family needed money for food.
- C Jane Whiting taught her how to beg.
- D She thought begging was a game.

4 What is a tippet?
- A an item of clothing
- B a trick
- C a small animal
- D a flower

5 What attitude did Mary Phillips have to the thieves when in court?
- A vicious
- B resentful
- C fair-minded
- C fearful

6 Why would the young Mary not have expected to be named 'a founding mother of early settlers of Australia' (lines 23–24)?

....

....

....

Answers and explanations on pages 111–112

SPELLING

Write the correct spelling of the underlined words in questions 1–4.

1 The charges were immediately dismisst.

2 Their sentence was transportstation.

3 Wailing expeditions were popular at the time.

4 The precise number of her decendents is uncertain.

5 Write three words from the word family that includes **accept**.

VOCABULARY

Circle the answers that have the nearest meaning to the underlined words in questions 6–7.

6 She gave her evidence in court.
A testimony B opinion
C facts D speech

7 Her sentence was changed to transportation to Australia.
A words B punishment
C doom D penalty

8 Add a word from the text to the sentence.

She had begged so often that it became .... nature to her.

9 Write a word from the text to match the meaning.

deposited as security for money borrowed, especially with a pawnbroker

Circle the word that does **not** belong.

10 A expedition B journey
C voyage D cruise

11 A probably B doubtless
C certainly D absolutely

GRAMMAR

12 Add a subjective adjective to the noun group.

The *Lady Juliana* was .... ship.
A a British B a wooden
C an uninteresting D a convict

13 Add a modal verb (e.g. must, will, can, should, could, might) to the verb group.

Do you think you .... be Mary's ancestor?

14 Complete the sentence with an adverbial from the text that tells **when**.

Mary sailed to Sydney ....

15 Circle the relative pronoun in the sentence and underline the noun group to which it refers.

Norfolk Island, which is off the coast of Australia, was settled by the British in 1788.

PUNCTUATION

Rewrite the sentences correctly.

16 mary wade was born on 5 october 1777

17 the surprise is a sailing ship that took mary to norfolk island

18 when she was 11 mary was tried in the old bailey a criminal court

Answers and explanations on page 112

TEXTS IN CONTEXT

 **Text 2**

Join a Tank Stream Tour

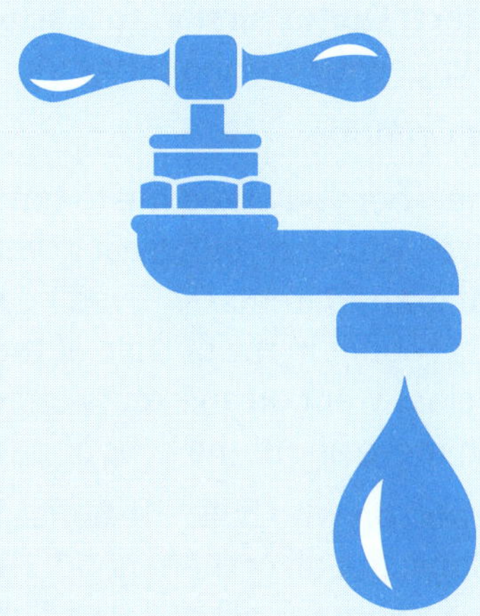

Soak up some history. You'll be in the safe hands of a guide who is knowledgeable about the history of the Tank Stream.

Take a journey—up close and personal—through 60 metres of heritage-listed tunnels built in the early years of the colony by convicts and stonemasons.

Learn what the Stream has meant to people over time.

Tours are available only twice a year. For more details about ticket sales, visit our homepage Tank Stream Tours at www.ttt.visit.com.

1 The purpose of Text 2 is to encourage

- **A** a love of history.
- **B** the sale of tickets.
- **C** understanding of the Tank Stream's importance.
- **D** interest in development plans.

2 Text 1 in Unit 4A is

- **A** an autobiography.
- **B** a narrative.
- **C** a biography.
- **D** an advertisement.

3 Where would you find the homepage for Tank Stream Tours?

- **A** in Wikipedia
- **B** on Twitter
- **C** on a website
- **D** in an email

4 'Tours are available only twice a year' (line 9) suggests that

- **A** tickets will be sought after and exclusive.
- **B** the tours aren't popular.
- **C** the company has run out of funding.
- **D** the company is understaffed.

5 Both illustrations are used

- **A** to represent ideas referred to in the texts.
- **B** to show what things in the text look like.
- **C** to record moments in history.
- **D** to explain what the texts are about.

6 Is Text 2 an effective piece of advertising? Why or why not?

....

....

....

....

Get creative

7 Visit the website The Proceedings of the Old Bailey: London's Central Criminal Court, 1674–1913 (www.oldbaileyonline.org/forms/formMain.jsp). Enter Mary Wade's name and the date of her trial. What is recorded there?

Answers and explanations on page 112

READING AND COMPREHENSION

Text 1

From: William@hereandnow.com
Subject: Our excursion to a historic house
To: wmlewis@cornholdings.uk

Dear Grandpa

Remember you asked me to tell you if we visited Vaucluse House? You said your great grandparents (my great-great-great-great grandparents???) lived near there when the house was being rebuilt in the middle of the 19th century. Well, yesterday our class went on an excursion to Vaucluse House—it has been a museum for over 100 years now—to learn more about the lives of people in Australia's colonial past.

The person who built the house was called William Charles Wentworth and he was famous for lots of reasons, not all of them good. He lived there with his wife, Sarah, and their ten children! They were called Thomasine (known as Timmie), William (Willie), Fanny, Fitzwilliam, Sarah (Joody), Eliza (Didy), Isabelle (Belle), Laura, Edith and D'Arcy. For some unknown reason, there were only three bedrooms for the ten children.

The house is very grand. It overlooks Sydney Harbour and has lots of turrets, arches and buttresses. We were told the grounds used to cover the whole of the suburb of Vaucluse but in 1911 the state government took back 23 acres so people could have access to the harbour foreshores. There are barracks for the servants (who were convicts), and a dairy, a scullery and huge kitchen, and a big vegetable garden. Of course they didn't have plumbing, power or electrical appliances back then so the servants must have worked very hard. There are stables with seven stalls and a coach house.

I had an audio tour of the house and learned lots of its secrets. I'll tell you some of them when you visit us at Christmas.

Love
William

1 Visitors to the house can now have a
- A tour with the owners.
- B virtual walkthrough.
- C audio tour.
- D imaginary tour.

2 How many rooms were there for the ten children?
- A 3
- B 5
- C 7
- D 9

3 William's comment—'not all of them good' (line 12)—is .... explained elsewhere in the text.
- A fully
- B partly
- C poorly
- D not

4 Why does William include the children's names?
- A to show they were once celebrities
- B to show off to his grandfather
- C to bring the children to life as individuals
- D to add extra historical facts

5 Choose **all** that apply. What made Vaucluse House grand?
- A the size of the grounds
- B the number of children
- C the servants who worked there
- D its elaborate architecture

6 What kind of relationship does William have with his grandfather?

Answers and explanations on page 112

SPELLING

Write the correct spelling of the underlined words in questions 1–4.

1 Vaucluse House is now a museeum.

....

2 The state goverment took back about 23 acres. ....

3 Do you have a vegeatable garden?

....

4 At that time, there was no plumming.

....

5 Write three words from the word family that includes **colonial**.

....

....

VOCABULARY

Circle the answers that have the nearest meaning to the underlined words in questions 6–7.

6 Wentworth was a famous figure in colonial Australia.

A popular B conspicuous
C well-known D extraordinary

7 We learned about Australia's colonial past.

A history B story
C activities D events

8 Add a word from the text to the sentence.

Vaucluse House no longer takes up the whole .... of Vaucluse.

9 Write a word from the text to match the meaning.

external supports built to steady a structure ....

Circle the word that does **not** belong.

10 A grand B splendid
C unusual D awe-inspiring

11 A buttress B turret
C house D arch

GRAMMAR

12 Add a subjective adjective to the noun group.

There were .... turrets on the building.

A impressive B three
C ornamented D brick

13 Add a modal verb (e.g. must, will, can, should, could, might) to the verb group.

You .... visit us at Christmas or we'll be very upset.

14 Complete the sentence with an adverbial from the text that tells **when**.

Vaucluse House was rebuilt ....

....

15 Circle the relative pronoun in the sentence and underline the noun group to which it refers.

They had lots of servants who worked very long hours.

PUNCTUATION

Rewrite the sentences correctly.

16 william billy and margaret meg are my cousins

....

....

17 the house has turrets arches and buttresses

....

....

18 my grandparents 25th grandchild has just been born

....

....

Answers and explanations on page 112

TEXTS IN CONTEXT

Text 2

William Charles Wentworth

William Charles Wentworth was born on Norfolk Island in 1793. His mother was a convict and his wife the child of convict parents. The stigma of this background meant his family was often snubbed by society. Nevertheless, Wentworth became well known as a successful explorer, barrister and author. His home, Vaucluse House, is now one of Sydney's Living Museums. Although he died when visiting England in 1872, he was given a state funeral and buried in a vault cut into rock in the grounds of Vaucluse House.

1 Text 2 can best be described as

- **A** a short autobiography.
- **B** a brief biography.
- **C** a reflection.
- **D** an exposition.

2 Text 1 in Unit 5A can best be described as

- **A** a personal email.
- **B** a historical email.
- **C** a business letter.
- **D** a personal webpage.

3 What was society's attitude towards Wentworth?

- **A** They looked down on him.
- **B** They admired his success.
- **C** They had mixed reactions to him.
- **D** They took no notice of him.

4 Why does William include question marks in the brackets in Text 1 (Unit 5A, line 7)?

- **A** to ask to be corrected if he has this calculation wrong
- **B** to show he's never met any of his great grandparents
- **C** to show he knows he has three lots of great-grandparents
- **D** to remind himself there are questions he wants to ask

5 Which words in Text 2 relate to the picture on the stamp?

- **A** convict
- **B** barrister
- **C** author
- **D** explorer

6 Why was it surprising that Wentworth was given a state funeral?

Get creative

7 Imagine you are one of Charles Wentworth's children. Write a letter to a schoolfriend about what you have been doing at home in the holidays.

Answers and explanations on pages 112–113

READING AND COMPREHENSION

 Text 1

The history of *The Three Bears*

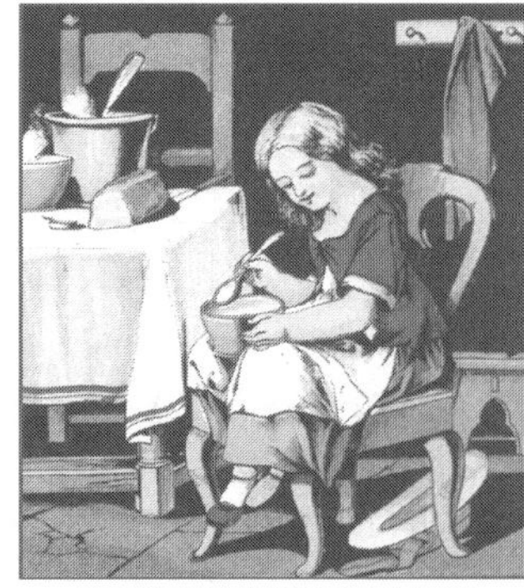

GOLDENHAIR EATS UP TINY-CUB'S PORRIDGE.

The Three Bears, published in 1837 by Robert Southey, is a written version of the story that made this fairytale famous. Southey (1774–1843) was an English poet, historian and biographer. He'd heard the story told by his uncle and had retold it to his own children. He thought it made an excellent tale for the nursery.

In his version there was a family of bears whom he called Little, Small, Wee Bear; Middle-sized Bear; and Great, Huge Bear. The person who invaded the house, when the bears were walking in the woods while their porridge cooled, was a little old woman 'who could not have been a good honest woman'. She went through the actions of tasting each bear's porridge, sitting in their chairs and trying out their beds. When the bears return and find her asleep in Little, Small, Wee Bear's bed, she jumps out of the window and escapes, never to be seen again. The author speculated that she might have been sent to a House of Correction.

Other versions of the story tell some parts quite differently. The intruder, for example, in a very early version was a fox named Scrapefoot. When she was found she was thrown out of the window by the bears. In others, as in Southey's version, she was a rather wicked little old woman who deserved to be punished severely. In later versions she became a child with curly hair that shone silver in the light earning herself the name Silver Hair or Silver Locks.

Eventually, in a 1904 version, she was described as a little girl with long, golden hair named Goldilocks and she has remained so ever since. Most modern versions end the story with Goldilocks escaping from the bears, who look on astonished when they realise their intruder is a golden-haired girl.

1 Who told Southey the story of *The Three Bears*?
- A his mother
- B his father
- C his uncle
- D his wife

2 In the caption the smallest bear is called
- A Wee Bear.
- B tiny-cub.
- C Little, Small, Wee Bear.
- D Baby Bear.

3 The bears are 'astonished' (line 22) because
- A they expected a fox.
- B they think of golden-haired girls as virtuous.
- C they expected a silver-haired girl.
- D they expected a golden-haired old woman.

4 The intruder changed over time from
- A a fox to Goldilocks.
- B a little old woman to a fox.
- C a silver-haired girl to a little old woman.
- D a golden-haired girl to a silver-haired girl.

5 The versions of the story are
- A similar in every way.
- B not at all similar.
- C unalike.
- D mainly similar but with some important differences.

6 Do you think the 'little old woman' in Southey's tale deserves to be punished severely? Explain your answer.

Answers and explanations on page 113

SPELLING

Write the correct spelling of the underlined words in questions 1–4.

1 Robert Southey's <u>vershion</u> of the story was popular. ....

2 I'm very fond of <u>fairytails</u>.

....

3 She didn't <u>desserve</u> that! ....

4 For a time, the <u>intruider</u> was called Silver Locks. ....

5 Write three words from the word family that includes **heard**.

....

....

VOCABULARY

Circle the answers that have the nearest meaning to the underlined words in questions 6–7.

6 Goldilocks was an <u>intruder</u> in the Bears' home.

A burglar | B trespasser
C squatter | D nuisance

7 The intruder was not a good, <u>honest</u> woman.

A reliable | B trustworthy
C sincere | D genuine

8 Add a word from the text to the sentence.

Her hair .... silver in the light.

9 Write a word from the text to match the meaning.

expressed an opinion without evidence or proof ....

Circle the word or word group that does **not** belong.

10 A escaping | B fleeing
C getting away | D standing

11 A thought | B said
C decided | D speculated

GRAMMAR

12 Add a subjective adjective to the noun group.

Goldilocks was .... girl.

A a charming
B a young
C an English
D a fair-haired

13 Add a modal verb (e.g. must, will, can, should, could, might) to the verb group.

I hope you .... find a picture of Goldilocks for me.

14 Complete the sentence with an adverbial from the text that tells **when**.

........................,

the intruder was named Goldilocks.

15 Circle the relative pronoun in the sentence and underline the noun group to which it refers.

The bears stared at the intruder, who was asleep in Baby Bear's bed.

PUNCTUATION

Rewrite the sentences correctly.

16 robert southey preferred the name little small wee bear

....

....

17 southey 1774–1843 was also famous as a poet

....

....

18 the three bears a fairy tale began as an oral tale

....

....

Answers and explanations on page 113

TEXTS IN CONTEXT

 **Text 2**

Fairytale cottage for sale

The home of the author of *The Three Bears,* Robert Southey, is up for sale. Burton Cottage, located in Dorset, is exactly the same on the outside as when Southey lived there. The inside has been modernised in a way that would satisfy anyone's dreams: the reception hall, the breakfast room, the kitchen and the bathroom are to die for. And then there's the cinema room! Not far away is the New Forest, where the three bears took their morning walk.

Phone now to make an appointment or visit our website (www.ftcottage.com.uk) for a visual tour of the property.

1 Text 2 is
- **A** a recount.
- **B** a narrative.
- **C** an exposition.
- **D** a discussion.

2 Text 1 in Unit 6A is primarily .... in emphasis.
- **A** historical
- **B** scientific
- **C** poetic
- **D** imaginative

3 Information included in Text 2
- **A** expands on topics referred to in Text 1.
- **B** is not related to Text 1.
- **C** is a modern version of Text 1.
- **D** is another version of the story of *The Three Bears.*

4 The information in Text 1 in Unit 6A is organised according to
- **A** the importance of the arguments.
- **B** the date of the versions.
- **C** causes and effects.
- **D** differences between versions of the tale.

5 The statement that the nearby forest is where the three bears walked is
- **A** credible.
- **B** untrue.
- **C** likely to be true.
- **D** a historical fact.

6 Would you like to buy the cottage that is for sale?

....

....

....

....

....

....

....

Get creative

7 Write a different ending for a version of *The Three Bears.*

Answers and explanations on page 113

Text 1

From 'The stones of five colours and the Empress Jokwa'

Long, long ago there lived a great Chinese Empress who succeeded her brother, the Emperor Fuki. It was the age of giants, and the Empress Jokwa, for that was her name, was 25 feet high [just over seven and a half metres], nearly as tall as her brother. She was a wonderful woman, and an able ruler. There is an interesting story of how she mended part of the broken heavens and one of the terrestrial pillars which upheld the sky, both of which were damaged during a rebellion raised by one of King Fuki's subjects.

The rebel's name was Kokai. He was 26 feet high. His body was entirely covered with hair, and his face was as black as iron. He was a wizard and a very terrible character indeed. When the Emperor Fuki died, Kokai was bitten with the ambition to be Emperor of China but his plan failed, and Jokwa, the dead Emperor's sister, mounted the throne. Kokai was so angry at being thwarted in his desire that he raised a revolt. His first act was to employ the Water Devil, who caused a great flood to rush over the country. This forced the poor people out of their homes and when the Empress Jokwa saw the plight of her subjects, and knew it was Kokai's fault, she declared war against him.

Jokwa, the Empress, had two young warriors called Hako and Eiko, and the former she made general of the front forces. Hako was delighted that the Empress's choice should fall on him, and he prepared himself for battle. He took up the longest lance he could find and mounted a red horse, and was just about to set out when he heard someone galloping hard behind him, shouting 'Hako! Stop! I must be the general of the front forces!'

Extract from 'The stones of five colours and the Empress Jokwa', *Japanese Fairy Tales*, compiled by Yei Theodora Ozaki, 1908. Available at www.gutenberg.org/files/4018/4018-h/4018-h.htm

1 Fuki was Jokwa's
- A cousin.
- B uncle.
- C brother.
- D son.

2 Who raised the rebellion against King Fuki?
- A Jokwa
- B Kokai
- C Hako
- D Eiko

3 How tall was Kokai in metres?
- A seven
- B about seven and a quarter
- C seven and a half
- D nearly eight

4 Why is Jokwa respected?
- A because of her height
- B because she helped save her people during the rebellion
- C because she was the Empress
- D because she made Hako a General

5 How does the author arouse the reader's anger against Kokai?
- A by describing his appearance
- B by saying he was a terrible character
- C by stating he was ambitious
- D by revealing his cruelty to others

6 What is likely to happen after Eiko stops Hako?

....

....

....

....

Answers and explanations on page 113

SPELLING

Write the correct spelling of the underlined words in questions 1–4.

1 The Umperor of China is very powerful. ……………

2 Jokwa was concerned about the plite of her people. ……………

3 Three terestial pillars hold up the sky. ……………

4 He heard a horse galoping towards him. ……………

5 Write three words from the word family that includes **choice**.

……………

……………

VOCABULARY

Circle the answers that have the nearest meaning to the underlined words in questions 6–7.

6 His plan was thwarted by her swift action.
A encouraged B tamed
C prevented D cramped

7 She was described as an able ruler.
A capable B brilliant
C straight D pleasing

8 Add a word from the text to the sentence.

Kokai decided to …………… the Water Devil to do his dirty work!

9 Write a word from the text to match the meaning.

an open rebellion; casting off loyalty to those in authority ……………

Circle the word that does **not** belong.

10 A cosmic B heavenly
C otherworldly D terrestrial

11 A aversion B ambition
C desire D longing

GRAMMAR

12 Add a subjective adjective to the noun group.

Hako mounted his …………… horse and prepared to gallop into battle.

A reddish-coloured
B brave
C newly groomed
D three-year-old

13 Add a modal verb (e.g. must, will, can, should, could, might) to the verb group.

'You …………… be punished for your evil deeds,' snarled the King.

14 Complete the sentence with an adverbial from the text that tells **when**.

This story happened ……………

…………….

15 Circle the relative pronoun in the sentence and underline the noun group to which it refers.

She punished the warrior, Kokai, who had betrayed his people.

PUNCTUATION

Rewrite the sentences correctly.

16 jokwa was the emperors sister

……………

……………

17 i am the new general hako shouted Eiko

……………

……………

18 he resented the empresss choice

……………

……………

Answers and explanations on page 114

TEXTS IN CONTEXT

Text 2

The Tallest Man

The Guinness Book of Records states that Robert Wadlow, at 2.72 metres, was the tallest man in history. Robert was born on 22 February 1918 in Alton, Illinois, USA. By the time he was eight he was taller than his father. At 13 he joined the boy scouts and had to have a specially made uniform, tent and sleeping bag. As a teenager he reached 2.45 metres, the tallest teenager ever. He continued to need specially made shoes and clothes as an adult. Robert was known for his kind and gentle nature, his humour and his willingness to take part in everything. When he was asked on radio if he was annoyed when people stared at him, he calmly replied, 'No, I just overlook them.'

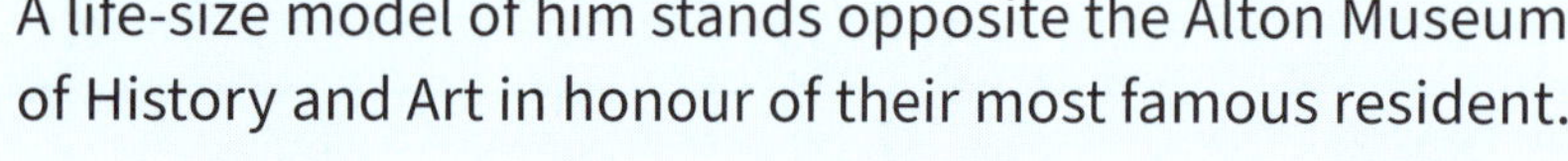

A life-size model of him stands opposite the Alton Museum of History and Art in honour of their most famous resident.

1 The purpose of Text 2 is to
- **A** tell the story of Wadlow's life.
- **B** describe what Wadlow looked like.
- **C** report on the tallest people in the world.
- **D** give information about the world's tallest man.

2 The purpose of Text 1 in Unit 7A is
- **A** to report historical events.
- **B** to tell a story of action and drama.
- **C** to explain how to deal with rebels.
- **D** to discuss what makes a good leader.

3 Choose **two** answers. Which words describe Text 1 in Unit 7A but not Text 2?
- **A** fantasy
- **B** non-fiction
- **C** fiction
- **D** informative

4 The writer's attitude to Kokai (Text 1, Unit 7A) is
- **A** neutral.
- **B** condemnatory.
- **C** unsympathetic.
- **D** approving.

5 The writer's attitude to Robert Wadlow in Text 2 is
- **A** admiring.
- **B** critical.
- **C** disapproving.
- **D** neutral.

6 What makes Wadlow's reply to the question he's asked (line 13) amusing?

....

....

....

....

7 Make a visual representation (drawing, painting, sculpture, etc.) of a character from Text 1 in Unit 7A.

Answers and explanations on page 114

Text 1

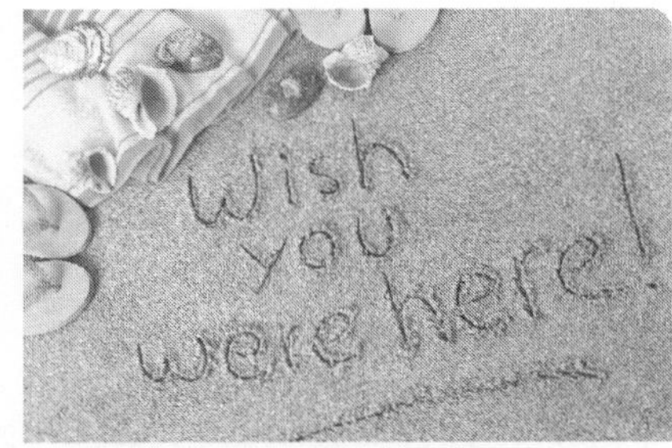

Postcard to Sally

Hi Sally

I really do wish you were here! Whoever heard of one twin breaking a leg while the other twin (not the other leg, haha, high five!) went on holiday?

Love

Charlie (PS I'll finish writing to you on paper now.)

So … when we first got to Auntie Jane's I was miserable without you and I sulked in my room. Dad persuaded me to give that up because he said I was spoiling his holiday and that I'd make Auntie Jane fed up if I didn't start enjoying myself. That made me feel guilty and now I'm having a much better time. I've met some other kids and we've been playing beach volleyball, which is great fun.

Auntie Jane is quite strict as you'll remember. Dad says she is a 'dark horse' and I should get to know her better. I think he might be right. When I sprained my wrist yesterday, she bandaged it for me and gave me a big bowl of strawberries from her garden with ice cream as well. She still has some of her favourite books she read as a child in her bookcase and she lets me borrow them. I'm reading *Alice in Wonderland* at the moment. It's about a girl who falls down a rabbit hole and finds herself in a wonderfully weird place! You should ask Mum to get it out of the library for you while you're stuck there in hospital.

Time for a swim (uh-oh, sorry Sally!!!) so I'd better go now. Do write back.

Love again!
Charlie

Text 2

Bakery bread

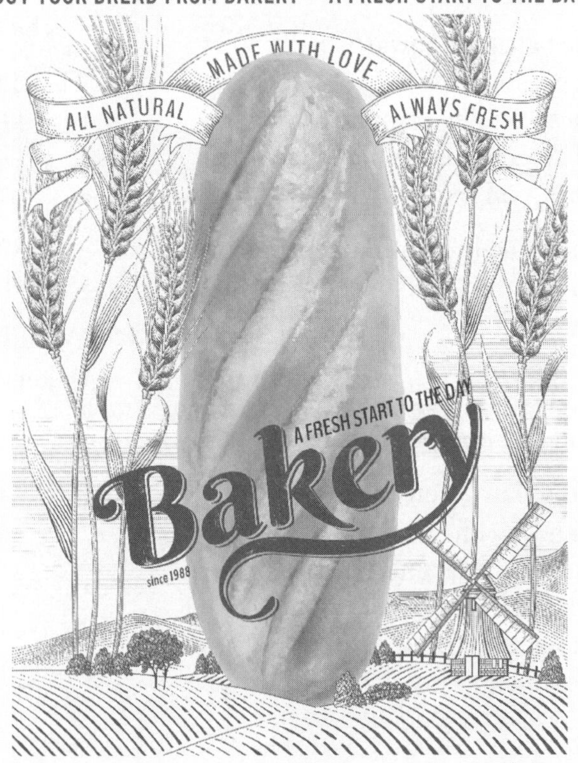

Read Text 1 on page 29 and then answer the questions.

1 Where is Charlie staying?
A at home
B with his mum
C at his Auntie Jane's
D at his dad's house

2 Why does Charlie write on paper as well as on the card?
A He ran out of space.
B He decided he wouldn't send the postcard.
C He had a big envelope to fill.
D Auntie Jane gave him some paper.

3 What does Charlie's joke (line 4) suggest?
A He is worried about Sally's other leg.
B He is not very good at telling jokes.
C He tells jokes whenever he gets the chance.
D He and Sally are used to sharing weak jokes.

4 Charlie apologises to Sally (line 18) because
A Sally is very strict with him.
B he knows Sally will be jealous.
C he feels he should write a longer message.
D he is surprised at how quickly time has passed.

5 What is Charlie's attitude towards Sally?
A bossy and a bit superior
B overdependent on her company
C very fond of her and misses being with her
D always showing off to her

6 How is Sally most likely to feel when she gets Charlie's postcard?
A mixed emotions
B extremely happy
C extremely sad
D confused and disappointed

7 What does Dad mean when he says Auntie Jane is a 'dark horse' (line 11)?
A Her skin has been darkened by the sun.
B There is a nasty side to her.
C She is easy to get to know.
D It takes time to get to know her fully.

8 How well does the image on the postcard suit Charlie's message? Explain.

....

....

....

....

Read Text 2 on page 29 and then answer the questions.

9 Text 2 is .... text.
A an explanatory
B a persuasive
C an informative
D a reflective

10 How is the word 'Bakery' made the most dominant word in the picture?
A It associates the name with home cooking.
B It is the name of the store where you can buy their products.
C It is placed in the forefront with the bread and background kept behind.
D It is more important than the picture of the bread.

11 The slogan 'a fresh start to the day' suggests bread from the Bakery
A is made from natural ingredients.
B is made with love.
C is fresh and will change your life.
D will never let you down.

12 Would you be likely to buy bread from the Bakery? Explain your answer.

....

....

....

....

....

Answers and explanations on page 114

Each sentence in questions 1–6 has one word that is incorrect. Write the correct spelling of each word in the boxes below.

1 I love birds, espeshally pelicans.

2 If we leave imediately, we'll make it in time.

3 Can you recommend a good restarant?

4 Its been centuries since that happened!

5 We visited Canberra when parlament was sitting.

6 She has a gilty conscience because she copied my homework.

7 Which word best matches the meaning of the underlined word?

Sarah realised the fossil she had found must be quite rare.

A sparse B limited
C strange D uncommon

8 Which word adds meaning to a noun in this sentence?

I looked through Mum's old photos to find some from when she was younger.

A through B old
C find D younger

9 In which sentence is **sound** used as a noun?
A That doesn't sound like Dad's voice.
B That loud sound is coming from the speakers.
C We had to learn to sound out our letters when we were in kindergarten.
D Would you sound out your parents to see if they'll let you come?

10 Which contraction correctly completes the sentence?

She said they .... going to come with us.

A wasn't B isn't C weren't D won't

11 Which verb group correctly completes the sentence?

.... you bought the fruit for our dessert yet?

A Shouldn't B Haven't
C Aren't D Mightn't

12 Which word group describes **when** the bird swooped?

At dawn the bird swooped down silently to finally catch the wriggly worm.

A At dawn B swooped down
C to finally D the wriggly worm

13 Which sentence shows the most certainty?
A Are you going to the cinema tomorrow?
B I definitely want to go to the cinema.
C Maybe we could go together?
D Mum will probably let me go if you're going.

14 Which word is the subject of this sentence?

After she'd watered the garden, Katrina decided to lie in her hammock.

A she'd B garden
C Katrina D hammock

15 Which word needs an apostrophe?

The dinosaurs eggs beneath those stones still have embryos inside their shells.

A dinosaurs B stones
C embryos D shells

16 Which sentence is punctuated correctly?
A 'Why cant you hear me, Mum?' I called.
B 'Why can't you hear me mum.' I called.
C 'Why can't you hear me, Mum' I called.
D 'Why can't you hear me, Mum?' I called.

Answers and explanations on page 114

 Text 1

New Year's resolutions

Dear Diary

Most people make New Year's resolutions at the beginning of the year. This year Mum resolved to learn yoga and Dad resolved to learn to be a better cook. I thought I would make a list on 1 January this year too but then I forgot! Now I see how well Mum and Dad are doing at their goals, I'm really impressed. So I've decided to make a list of my resolutions right now. I'll start working on it very soon. Better late than never, I say.

I'm going to:

1 help Grandpa learn to use the voice app on his computer
2 get a paper run and save up
3 teach Mum to forget to tell me when it's my bedtime
4 learn how to make pancakes for breakfast
5 call people (especially Auntie Ruth) to say thank you for their cards or presents immediately instead of forgetting for weeks and weeks
6 find a new hobby and become expert at it
7 convince Dad I would not forget to look after a guinea pig if only he'd let me have one
8 learn martial arts so I can defend myself
9 be a really good friend to Mike and Susie
10 practise my gymnastic sequences and remember to go to training
11 improve my Maths marks by working harder.

I've put a lot of goals down because that way I'll have lots of choice.

Talk to you tomorrow
Sabrina

1 Who wrote the 11 resolutions?
A Sabrina's mum
B Sabrina's dad
C Auntie Ruth
D Sabrina

2 What has impressed Sabrina?
A her mum's list of resolutions
B how well her mum and dad are doing at their goals
C her dad's resolutions
D the number of goals she thinks of

3 Which goal of Sabrina's is a bit of a joke
A 1 B 3 C 7 D 10

4 What is Sabrina good at?
A using technology B cooking
C martial arts D Maths

5 Choose **all** that apply. Sabrina is
A forgetful at times.
B mostly well-meaning.
C hopeless at most things.
D impolite and cheeky.

6 How likely do you think it is that Sabrina will keep her resolutions? Explain.

Answers and explanations on page 115

SPELLING

Rewrite the misspelt words in questions 1–4.

1 That was my gaol this year, too!

2 People usually make resolutions at the begining of the year.

3 I practice gym every day after school.

4 She keeps a dairy to write down her memories.

5 Write three words from the word family that includes **improve**.

VOCABULARY

Circle the answers that have the nearest meaning to the underlined words in questions 6–7.

6 She resolved to find a new hobby before the day was over.

A fixed B hoped
C determined D wanted

7 I use my voice app to send texts.

A speech B computer
C statements D broadcasting

8 Add a word from the text to the sentence.

I want to work harder so my marks will .

9 Write a word from the text to match the meaning.

without delay; instantly; at once

Circle the word that does **not** belong.

10 A recall B ignore
C remember D recollect

11 A skilled B adept
C inexperienced D expert

GRAMMAR

12 Add a subjective adjective to the noun group.

If only I had a guinea pig!

A lovable B baby
C pet D tame

13 Name the tense of the underlined verb.

I promise I will keep my resolutions next year.

14 Complete the sentence with an adverbial from the text that tells **how**.

I hope to improve my Maths marks .

15 Circle the relative pronoun in the sentence and underline the noun group to which it refers.

My friend, for whom I made some pancakes, gobbled them all up!

PUNCTUATION

Rewrite the sentences correctly.

16 what are your new years resolutions asked sabrina

17 im pleased im going to visit grandpa

18 ive written my goals for this year already

Answers and explanations on page 115

 Text 2

Caring for your guinea pig

1 Line your guinea pig's cage with paper for its bedding and change this daily.

2 Make sure your guinea pig always has fresh, clean water.

3 Provide soft hay in the cage to keep the guinea pig's digestive tract healthy.

4 Feed your guinea pig about a cup full of vegetables each day. Get a list from your pet shop as to which vegetables are suitable.

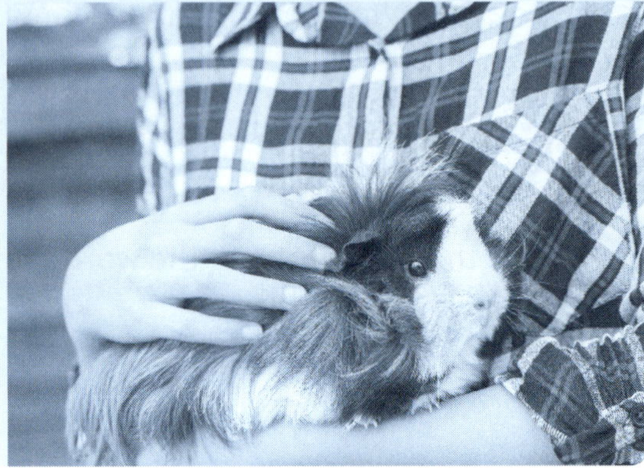

5 Let your guinea pig have time to run about in a safe place each day. Provide toys for it to play with.

6 Groom your guinea pig regularly and remember to cut its toenails every three weeks or so.

1 What is the purpose of Text 2?

- **A** to describe a guinea pig's day
- **B** to explain why guinea pigs make good pets
- **C** to tell how to look after a guinea pig
- **D** to list things you can do with guinea pigs

2 What is the purpose of Text 1 in Unit 8A?

- **A** to express personal thoughts
- **B** to promote making resolutions
- **C** to describe Sabrina's diary
- **D** to discuss different points of view

3 Text 2 lists things the author thinks you

- **A** could do.
- **B** will do.
- **C** won't do.
- **D** must do.

4 Choose **all** that apply. Which statements are true?

- **A** The author of Text 2 writes in a relaxed, friendly way.
- **B** The author of Text 1 in Unit 8A writes in a relaxed, friendly way.
- **C** The author of Text 1 in Unit 8A writes in a confident, authoritative way.
- **D** The author of Text 2 writes in a confident, authoritative way.

5 What makes the reader trust the advice given in Text 2?

....

....

....

....

6 If Sabrina (Text 1, Unit 8A) had a guinea pig for a pet, would she look after it properly? Explain.

....

....

....

....

Get creative

7 Make your own list of New Year's resolutions. Follow Sabrina's format.

Answers and explanations on page 115

 Text 1

To the naturalist

Portrait of Watkin Tench, unknown

To the naturalist this country holds out many invitations. Birds, though not remarkably numerous, are in great variety, and of the most exquisite beauty of plumage, among which are the cockatoo, lory, and parroquet; but the bird which principally claims attention is a species of ostrich … One of them was shot, at a considerable distance, with a single ball, by a convict employed for that purpose by the Governor … Though incapable of flying, they run with such swiftness, that our fleetest greyhounds are left far behind in every attempt to catch them. The flesh was eaten, and tasted like beef.

Of the natural history of the kangaroo we are still very ignorant. We may, however, venture to pronounce this animal, a new species of opossum, the female being furnished with a bag, in which the young is contained; and in which the teats are found. These last are only two in number, a strong presumptive proof, had we no other evidence, that the kangaroo brings forth rarely more than one at a birth.

After this perhaps I shall hardly be credited, when I affirm that the kangaroo on being brought forth is not larger than an English mouse. It is, however, in my power to speak positively on this head, as I have seen more than one instance of it.

… Sharks of an enormous size are found here. One of these was caught by the people on board the *Sirius*, which measured at the shoulders six feet and a half in circumference. His liver yielded twenty-four gallons of oil …

Venomous animals and reptiles are rarely seen. Large snakes beautifully variegated have been killed, but of the effect of their bites we are happily ignorant.

Extract from Chapter XV of *A Narrative of the Expedition to Botany Bay* by Watkin Tench, 1788
www.gutenberg.org/files/3535/3535-h/3535-h.htm

1 Which bird is incapable of flying?
- A cockatoo
- B lory
- C perroquet
- D ostrich

2 Who painted Tench's portrait?
- A a convict
- B a naturalist
- C nobody knows
- D Watkin Tench

3 Why is Tench ignorant of the natural history of the kangaroo?
- A He has never seen one.
- B The English hadn't been long in Botany Bay.
- C The information is in Britain.
- D He hadn't bothered to find out about it.

4 What is the main source of Tench's information?
- A other travellers
- B Aboriginal trackers
- C his own observations
- D what the convicts reported to him

5 Tench finds the natural world around Botany Bay
- A impressive.
- B frightening.
- C disturbing.
- D peculiar.

6 Is Tench a trustworthy narrator? Explain.

Answers and explanations on page 115

SPELLING

Rewrite the misspelt words in questions 1–4.

1 Naturalists are interested in the naturel world.

2 The colours of the parrot are exquizate.

3 That is a different speecies of bird.

4 Did you measure its circumfrense?

5 Write three words from the word family that includes **attention**.

VOCABULARY

Circle the answers that have the nearest meaning to the underlined words in questions 6–7.

6 The babies are contained in their mother's pouch.
A held B embraced
C seated D released

7 We were ignorant about the ways of many of these animals.
A uninformed B dense
C birdbrained D useless

8 Add a word from the text to the sentence.
I can ______ that a baby kangaroo is very tiny.

9 Write a word from the text to match the meaning.
a person who studies or is an expert in natural history, especially a zoologist or botanist

Circle the word that does **not** belong.

10 A mottled B streaked
C unvaried D variegated

11 A fleetest B sleekest
C fastest D quickest

GRAMMAR

12 Add a subjective adjective to the noun group.
The lory has ______ plumage.
A exquisite B multicoloured
C damaged D variegated

13 Name the tense of the underlined verb.
She said we might see a baby kangaroo if we were patient but they usually stayed hidden.

14 Complete the sentence with an adverbial from the text that tells **how**.
The convict shot the ostrich ______.

15 Circle the relative pronoun in the sentence and underline the noun group to which it refers.
The brown-bellied snake, which was hiding in a log, was venomous.

PUNCTUATION

Rewrite the sentences correctly.

16 we did however decide to travel further

17 did you sail on the sirius from england

18 the books title is a narrative of the expedition to botany bay

Answers and explanations on page 115

Text 2

King George's Sound

King George's Sound is a large ocean inlet on the south coast of Western Australia. It was originally inhabited by Aboriginal tribes, who told Dreamtime stories about the three Noongar tribes of the area who lived there when the water was one big harbour and not three as it is today. They believed giant lizards from the Dreaming found a way to stop the tribes fighting by lying down in the water and dividing it into three sections.

When George Vancouver, an English explorer, landed there in 1791 he named the area after King George III. Others to visit the Sound in the early part of the 19th century include Matthew Flinders in 1801–2 on *HMS Investigator* and Charles Darwin in 1836 on the *Beagle*.

© Fctdolas, WikiCommons

1 The purpose of Text 2 is to
- A persuade.
- B explain.
- C inform.
- D narrate.

2 Text 1 in Unit 9A presents
- A an Aboriginal view of Australian animals.
- B a British view of Australian animals.
- C a British view of English animals.
- D an unknown view of British and Australian animals.

3 Text 2 presents information in
- A a time sequence.
- B random order.
- C a causal sequence.
- D a mathematical sequence.

4 Text 2 mainly presents a series of
- A opinions.
- B judgements.
- C facts.
- D personal views.

5 The writer of Text 1 in Unit 9A tends to
- A justify his opinions.
- B exaggerate his facts.
- C use poetic language.
- D use emotive language.

6 Do the writers of Text 1 in Unit 9A and Text 2 have the same attitude to their subjects? Explain.

....

....

....

7 Draw, paint or sculpt a picture of something referred to in either of the texts.

Answers and explanations on pages 115–116

READING AND COMPREHENSION

 Text 1

Daisy Duck takes off

And to end our bulletin we bring you rather special news about a duck whose life has suddenly taken a turn for the better—thanks to our local primary school.

It all began when Daisy Duck lost her foot. No-one really knows how this happened but lose her foot she did. Mr and Mrs Fluff, her owners, think it was bitten off by their tortoise who is known to get rather snappy at times. Mr Right, their next-door neighbour, fears he may unintentionally have run over Daisy's foot with his tractor. And the Fluffs' dog looks guilty every time Daisy wobbles past.

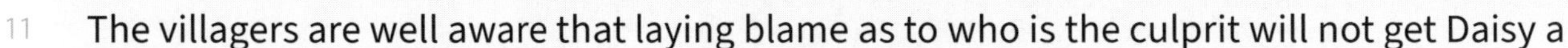

The villagers are well aware that laying blame as to who is the culprit will not get Daisy a new foot. The vet has done her best. She's given her antibiotics to make sure no infection develops and she's bound up her leg as best she can. But the life of a duck who has to wobble and bumble her way around and cannot do things other ducks do such as flying, swimming and running is a difficult one.

Enter the caring children of our local primary school. With the help of their teachers, a group of concerned students made Daisy a new foot. They used their new 3D printer to fashion a foot that could be fitted onto her leg. It took a great deal of trial and error but they persevered with their efforts. It also took Daisy quite a while to get used to her new foot but now she can run quite quickly and is extremely pleased with herself. Mr Avian, a spokesperson for the school, said the children have plans to make Daisy a second foot that she can wear when swimming. Well done, Leeland Primary. Keep up the good work.

1 What did Daisy lose?
- A her owner
- B the vet
- C her temper
- D her foot

2 The Fluffs think Daisy's foot was
- A run over by a tractor.
- B snapped off by a dog.
- C bitten off by a tortoise.
- D damaged by some children.

3 Where would you hear this text?
- A on local radio
- B at the school hall
- C on national television
- D on a CD about ducks

4 The text is an example of
- A a cautionary tale.
- B a reality tv show.
- C a feel-good news story.
- D made-up news.

5 Choose **all** that apply. The students of Leeland Primary showed
- A impatience.
- B concern.
- C initiative.
- D persistence.

6 The attitude of the speaker to the story is
- A nostalgic.
- B critical.
- C standoffish.
- D congratulatory.

Answers and explanations on page 116

SPELLING

Rewrite the misspelt words in questions 1–4.

1 Who is gilty? ....

2 Are you the culpret? ....

3 He is the spokespersen for the school.

....

4 The class felt conserned for the duck.

....

5 Write three words from the word family that includes **unintentional**.

....

....

....

VOCABULARY

Circle the answers that have the nearest meaning to the underlined words in questions 6–7.

6 They <u>persevered</u> with their efforts.
- A maintained
- B persisted
- C lasted
- D proceeded

7 You could tell the duck felt <u>extremely</u> pleased.
- A quite
- B excessively
- C extraordinarily
- D willingly

8 Add a word from the text to the sentence.

There's no point in .... blame as it won't solve the problem.

9 Write a word from the text to match the meaning.

chemical substances that can kill bacteria

....

Circle the word that does **not** belong.

10
- A infection
- B virus
- C germ
- D measles

11
- A concerned
- B anxious
- C satisfied
- D worried

GRAMMAR

12 Add a subjective adjective to the noun group.

Daisy has a .... new foot.
- A prosthetic
- B groovy
- C plastic
- D 3D-printed

13 Name the tense of the underlined verb group.

The vet <u>had done</u> her very best.

....

14 Complete the sentence with an adverbial from the text that tells **how**.

Mr Right thinks he ran over Daisy's foot

....

15 Circle the relative pronoun in the sentence and underline the noun group to which it refers.

A new, prosthetic foot was made for Daisy who had lost a foot of her own.

PUNCTUATION

Rewrite the sentences correctly.

16 daisy a duck with a missing foot is in hospital

....

....

17 well done everyone she said

....

....

18 that girls dog is looking guilty

....

....

Answers and explanations on page 116

TEXTS IN CONTEXT

Text 2

3D printing is changing the world

3D printing uses a digital model to create 3D objects. The materials used, such as heated plastic or powders, are layered and fed into the machine which then produces the parts needed to make the desired objects. Medicine is a field using this procedure where big advances have been made. For example, prosthetic limbs are now being customised for individuals and at a much lower cost than in the past.

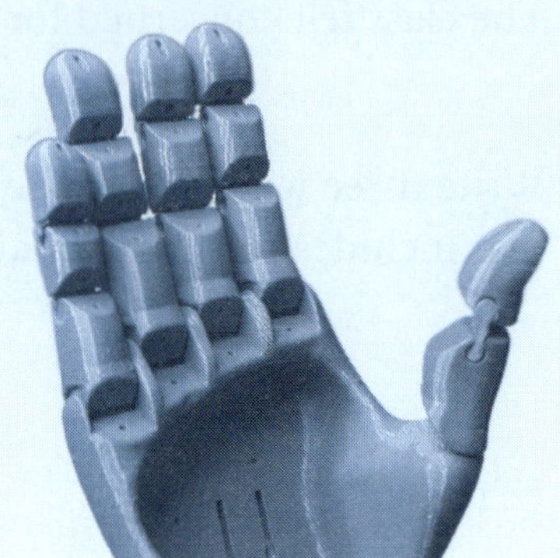

A recent project called e-NABLE, a non-profit community supported project, is providing young children who need a new hand with a 3D plastic, printed robotic hand—for free. Holding a ball or a bike handle is no longer just a dream for these children. Whatever next?

1. The purpose of Text 2 is to
   - **A** encourage people to buy 3D printers.
   - **B** persuade people to donate to e-NABLE.
   - **C** report on what 3D printers can do.
   - **D** encourage the start-up of a non-profit company.

2. The title of Text 1 in Unit 10A suggests that what follows will be
   - **A** entertaining.
   - **B** persuasive.
   - **C** overwhelming.
   - **D** distressing.

3. Where would you be **unlikely** to read Text 2?
   - **A** in a newspaper
   - **B** in a magazine
   - **C** in an article
   - **D** in junk mail

4. Which statements are true? Choose **all** that apply.
   - **A** Text 1 in Unit 10A gives some general information about 3D printers.
   - **B** Text 1 in Unit 10A tells a story about what a particular 3D printer was used for.
   - **C** Text 2 tells a story about what a particular 3D printer was used for.
   - **D** Text 2 gives some general information about 3D printers.

5. Text 1 in Unit 10A is mainly .... while Text 2 is mainly .... in tone.
   - **A** lighthearted/serious
   - **B** serious/lighthearted
   - **C** hilarious/amusing
   - **D** formal/informal

6. Does Text 2 convince you that 3D printers are changing the world? Explain your answer.

   ....

   ....

   ....

   ....

   ....

   ....

7. Find out some other things 3D printers can be used to make.

Answers and explanations on page 116

READING AND COMPREHENSION

Text 1

Albert Namatjira (1902–1959)

Albert (Elea) Namatjira was born in 1902 in Hermannsburg (Ntaria), an Aboriginal community in Central Australia. He was given the name Albert when his family joined the Lutheran Church in 1905. Except for six months during his 13th year, Albert attended the Mission school until he was 18. The six months was spent in the bush where he had his initiation learning traditional Aboriginal laws and customs.

In Aboriginal culture, boys are initiated into manhood through a cycle of ceremonies. They learn songs and perform dances from the Dreamtime and take part in secret sacred rituals. This experience would have strengthened Namatjira's close ties with, and knowledge of, the landscape of his people.

As a boy and young man, Albert enjoyed sketching things in his surroundings—cattle, stockmen, and so on—and carving and decorating boomerangs, woomeras and plaques. When well-known European artists exhibited their work in the area, Namatjira was fascinated by their paintings of the landscapes he knew so well. After working at various jobs as a carpenter, blacksmith and cameleer, Namatjira decided to learn more about painting so he could become an artist. It was not long before he was having successful exhibitions of his watercolours and went on to complete around 2000 artworks.

In time, Namatjira's paintings brought him fame. He was hailed as the first Aboriginal painter to paint in a modern European style. Yet his work also carries characteristics of traditional Aboriginal art such as repetition, patterning and placing the horizon high in the picture.

As an Aboriginal person, Namatjira was not allowed to lease property or own land even though he became an Australian celebrity. This changed when the government granted him and his wife full Australian citizenship—the first Aboriginal people to receive this.

1 Namatjira was born in
- A the Lutheran Church.
- B Hermannsburg.
- C the bush.
- D Europe.

2 Namatjira worked occasionally as a
- A singer.
- B plumber.
- C lawyer.
- D cameleer.

3 The formal education of Namatjira was carried out by
- A the Lutheran Mission school.
- B his parents.
- C his Aboriginal tribe.
- D European artists.

4 Namatjira's ties with the landscape .... his painting.
- A had no impact on
- B hindered
- C enriched
- D interrupted

5 What was the catalyst that sparked Namatjira's artistic career?
- A his initiation
- B his schooling
- C seeing exhibitions by European artists
- D gaining Australian citizenship

6 Why might Namatjira's face have been put on a stamp in 1968?

....

 ....

Answers and explanations on page 116

SPELLING

Rewrite the misspelt words in questions 1–4.

1 He took part in a cycel of ceremonies.

2 His paintings were shown in many exibitions.

3 I like the decoration on that whoomera.

4 What are the characteristicks of his style?

5 Write three words from the word family that includes **Aboriginal**.

VOCABULARY

Circle the answers that have the nearest meaning to the underlined words in questions 6–7.

6 The ceremonies include sacred rituals.

A irreligious
B unholy
C solemn
D spiritual

7 He worked at various occupations.

A different
B several
C few
D numerous

8 Add a word from the text to the sentence.

What happens at initiation ceremonies is mostly kept .

9 Write a word from the text to match the meaning.

the state of being vested with the rights, privileges and duties of a citizen

Circle the word that does **not** belong.

10 A characteristics
B standards
C qualities
D features

11 A bigwig
B celebrity
C VIP
D nonentity

GRAMMAR

12 Add a subjective adjective to the noun group.

Namatjira was known for his paintings.

A colourful
B dreamy
C landscape
D watercolour

13 Name the tense of the underlined verb groups.

I am hoping Dad will buy me a ticket.

14 Complete the sentence with an adverbial from the text that tells **how**.

Boys are initiated into manhood .

15 Circle the relative pronoun in the sentence and underline the noun group to which it refers.

They admired Namatjira who later became quite famous.

PUNCTUATION

Rewrite the sentences correctly.

16 was he born in an aboriginal community

17 they performed dances from dreamtime stories

18 in time namatjira became famous

Answers and explanations on pages 116–117

TEXTS IN CONTEXT

Text 2

Indigenous winner for 2020 Archibald

❶ Vincent Namatjira, great-grandson of Albert Namatjira, has won this year's Archibald Prize for portrait painting.

❷ Vincent's great-grandfather was the subject of a portrait by William Dargie that won the prize in 1956. The Archibald, however, has not been won by an Indigenous Australian in its 99-year history. Namatjira's paintings have now been among the finalists for the prize four years in a row.

❸ The winning painting, *Stand strong for who you are*, is a double portrait of the artist shaking hands with Adam Goodes, a former AFL football legend. Behind these figures, he paints Goodes in poses that recall moments when he was making a stand against bullying and racism.

❹ Some describe Namatjira's style as 'raw and untrained' while others see it as 'witty, startling and honest'.

1 Text 2 is
- **A** an autobiography.
- **B** a biography.
- **C** a news article.
- **D** a review.

2 Text 1 in Unit 11A is
- **A** an autobiography.
- **B** a biography.
- **C** a news article.
- **D** a review.

3 In which paragraph of Text 2 is there information that could be added to Albert Namatjira's story (Text 1, Unit 11A)?
- **A** paragraph one
- **B** paragraph two
- **C** paragraph three
- **D** paragraph four

4 The title of Namatjira's painting, *Stand strong for who you are*, suggests it is about
- **A** health and safety matters.
- **B** personal values.
- **C** racist attitudes.
- **D** the relation of past and present.

5 What is the author's attitude in Text 2 to Namatjira's style?
- **A** neutral
- **B** opposed
- **C** approving
- **D** critical

6 Name **two** things that would be likely to surprise Albert Namatjira if he were to read Text 2.

....

....

....

....

Get creative

7 Find out more about Vincent Namatjira's art. Do you like his paintings? Why or why not?

Answers and explanations on page 117

Text 1

A special friend

If you're looking for a special friend you should find an old lady.

Adie must be nearly 100 and she is just about perfect for a friend. Of course, she can't run. She's got one of those built-up shoes because one of her legs is shorter than the other. But she can keep secrets and she lets me eat slices of cheese, spread with jam on both sides.

She has all sorts of things that other friends don't. There's a big drawer in her bedroom that has just about everything in it. Sometimes she lets me tip everything out so I can play with the contents while she sits on her bed darning her stockings. Mum says she hoards things but I don't tell Adie in case it hurts her feelings.

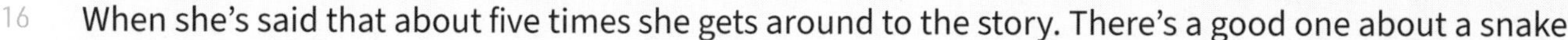

I often ask her to tell me a story and she always says,

'Alright. About Jack A'Magorey. Will I begin it?'

'Yes.'

'Well, that's all that's in it.'

When she's said that about five times she gets around to the story. There's a good one about a snake that slid under the front door. A girl called Patsy thought it was a skipping rope and picked it up to skip with it. Adie came to the rescue by knocking it from Patsy's hands and standing on it with her big black shoe. I don't know how she got on before she got that shoe.

Anyway, my advice is to check through your rellies until you find an old lady who'd make a good friend. If Adie is anything to go by, they make the very best kind.

by Ally

1. Who does Ally suggest you find for a friend?
   - A Adie
   - B Patsy
   - C Jack
   - D an old lady

2. Adie's story is about
   - A Jack.
   - B a snake.
   - C a big drawer.
   - D keeping secrets.

3. Why is Adie such an unusual choice of friend?
   - A She has a built-up shoe.
   - B She can't run.
   - C She's so much older than Ally.
   - D She tells stories.

4. The words 'I don't tell Adie in case it hurts her feelings' (lines 10–11) suggest that Ally
   - A is sensitive and thoughtful.
   - B often tells untruths.
   - C knows which side her bread is buttered.
   - D pretends to be fond of Adie.

5. What kind of person is Adie? Choose **all** that apply.
   - A patient
   - B kind
   - C loyal
   - D strict

6. Would you like to have Ally as a friend? Why or why not?

....

....

....

....

....

Answers and explanations on page 117

SPELLING

Rewrite the misspelt words in questions 1–4.

1 I think she is the purfect friend.

2 My friend hordes pencils and pens in her cupboard.

3 She spred my cheese with jam!

4 It tasted rather speshial.

5 Write three words from the word family that includes **thought**.

VOCABULARY

Circle the answers that have the nearest meaning to the underlined words in questions 6–7.

6 She is perfect to have as a friend.
- A ideal
- B expert
- C accomplished
- D clever

7 Sometimes we have breakfast together.
- A Rarely
- B Constantly
- C Occasionally
- D Always

8 Add a word from the text to the sentence.

If you are unkind you can hurt people's ______________.

9 Write a word from the text to match the meaning.

exceptional; particularly valued

Circle the word that does **not** belong.

10
- A lends
- B collects
- C accumulates
- D hoards

11
- A slipped
- B slithered
- C glided
- D accelerated

GRAMMAR

12 Add a subjective adjective to the noun group.

It was a ______________ snake.
- A brown
- B venomous
- C patterned
- D nasty

13 Name the tense of the underlined verbs.

Adie came to the rescue when the snake slid under the door.

14 Complete the sentence with an adverbial from the text that tells **how**.

Adie stood on the snake ______________.

15 Circle the relative pronoun in the sentence and underline the noun group to which it refers.

My friend, whom I love dearly, made us all pancakes for breakfast.

PUNCTUATION

Rewrite the sentences correctly.

16 of course she cant keep a secret

17 well thats all thats in it

18 anyway thats my advice

Answers and explanations on page 117

Text 2

Time to talk

When a friend calls to me from the road
And slows his horse to a meaning walk,
I don't stand still and look around
On all the hills I haven't hoed,
And shout from where I am, What is it?
No, not as there is a time to talk.
I thrust my hoe in the mellow ground,
Blade-end up and five feet tall,
And plod: I go up to the stone wall
For a friendly visit.

by Robert Frost, 1920

Source: www.gutenberg.org/files/29345/29345-h/29345-h.htm#A_TIME_TO_TALK

1 Text 2 is
- **A** a play.
- **B** a poem.
- **C** a short story.
- **D** an extract from a novel.

2 In Text 2 the author
- **A** reflects on his own behaviour.
- **B** criticises a friend's actions.
- **C** explains his problems.
- **D** describes a visitor.

3 The main theme of both Text 1 in Unit 12A and Text 2 is
- **A** the usefulness of stories.
- **B** the value of friendship.
- **C** the pleasure of wasting time.
- **D** the difficulty of solving problems.

4 Both Text 1 in Unit 12A and Text 2
- **A** are conversational in tone.
- **B** have a rural setting.
- **C** use rhyme and rhythm to create a mood.
- **D** are full of humour.

5 How suitable is the picture for Text 2? Explain.

....

....

....

....

6 Which text do you prefer? Explain.

....

....

....

....

....

Get creative

7 Write a diary entry or a poem called **Friends**.

Answers and explanations on pages 117–118

READING AND COMPREHENSION

Text 1

The elephant

The elephant is the largest living land mammal. Unsurprisingly it spends between 12 and 18 hours eating and drinking. It consumes large quantities of grasses, leaves, bamboo, bark, roots and other vegetation, and drinks an average-sized bathtub full of water. An elephant does not have a very efficient digestive system and as a consequence produces large quantities of manure!

Elephants live in herds made up of family groups, usually of about eight to ten related females. These are led by the oldest female, the matriarch. When necessary, a matriarch will rely on the elephant's excellent memory to guide its herds to watering holes that have been visited in the past. The calves, usually one per elephant born after a 22-month gestation period, are cared for by the mother and other close females. When a male calf is somewhere between 12 and 15 years old, it leaves the group and usually lives a fairly solitary life.

The trunk of an elephant has multiple functions and is one of its most distinctive features. It uses it to breathe (its nostrils run the length of its trunk), feed, smell, bring water to its mouth and spray it over its body. The trunk can sense vibrations coming towards it from a distance. It is strong enough to push down trees or lift extremely heavy weights. It is able to pick up both large and small things and to reach things at quite a distance. The trunk is used for greetings and caresses and plays an important part in the way elephants communicate with each other.

Some species of elephant are now extinct but three species—the African bush elephant, the African forest elephant and the Asian elephant—currently survive in the savannahs, forests, deserts and marshy areas of Africa and Asia.

1 Elephant herds are made up of
- A males and females.
- B related females.
- C related males.
- D males, females and babies.

2 How many species of elephant are not extinct?
- A one
- B two
- C three
- D four

3 Elephants produce lots of manure because
- A they are fussy eaters.
- B they are greedy eaters.
- C they eat too much meat.
- D their digestive systems are not very effective.

4 An elephant's trunk
- A has two short nostrils.
- B is not very strong.
- C is mainly used for display.
- D is immensely useful.

5 The social behaviour of the elephant herd is .... that of humans.
- A the same as
- B different from
- C similar to
- D unrelated to

6 What makes the matriarch a good leader of a herd?

....

 ....

Answers and explanations on page 118

SPELLING

Rewrite the misspelt words in questions 1–4.

1 Their memories are extreamly good.

2 That's a very long guestation period.

3 The elephant can comunicate with its trunk.

4 Its digestive system is inefishient.

5 Write three words from the word family that includes **sense**.

VOCABULARY

Circle the answers that have the nearest meaning to the underlined words in questions 6–7.

6 Their trunks have multiple functions.
A a few B many
C occasional D single

7 Some species will not survive unless things improve.
A last B subsist
C respond D depart

8 Add a word from the text to the sentence.

The oldest female elephant is the ______ of the herd.

9 Write a word from the text to match the meaning.

performing or functioning in the best possible manner with the least waste of time and effort

Circle the word that does **not** belong.

10 A solitary B alone
C accompanied D solo

11 A stillness B tremors
C movements D vibrations

GRAMMAR

12 Add a subjective adjective to the noun group.

They drank from a ______ stream.
A welcoming B flooding
C half-empty D stagnant

13 Name the tense of the underlined verb.

The elephant is the largest land mammal.

14 Complete the sentence with an adverbial from the text that tells **how**.

The new-born calf was cared for ______.

15 Circle the relative pronoun in the sentence and underline the noun group to which it refers.

The matriarch, who is wise and experienced, is leader of the herd.

PUNCTUATION

Rewrite the sentences correctly.

16 elephants eat grass leaves and other vegetation

17 the calves one per elephant are born a day apart

18 they live in savannahs forests deserts and marshy areas

Answers and explanations on page 118

TEXTS IN CONTEXT

 Text 2

Ivory poaching

Elephants' tusks are their continuously growing front teeth! The visible part of the tusk, the ivory, has always been in high demand. Over time, poaching of elephants to illegally gain ivory has led to the destruction of hundreds of thousands of elephants. The cruel methods used to kill these magnificent animals include shooting prey from helicopters or using machetes and spears spiked with cyanide.

In 1989, CITES (Convention on International Trade in Endangered Species of Wild Fauna and Flora) introduced a ban on the international trading of ivory. This had some protective effects, as did the Chinese and American Presidents enacting ivory bans in their own countries. However, poaching and illegal trafficking of ivory appears to have gained ground again and is currently contributing to the endangerment of some species.

1. What is the purpose of Text 2?
   - **A** to tell people about the failure of CITES
   - **B** to persuade people that ivory poaching is harmless
   - **C** to give information about the history of ivory poaching
   - **D** to describe what elephants' tusks look like

2. Text 1 in Unit 13A is
   - **A** an exposition.
   - **B** an information report.
   - **C** a discussion.
   - **D** a review.

3. Which statement is **not** a fact?
   - **A** Ivory poaching has contributed to the deaths of many elephants.
   - **B** Elephants are herbivores.
   - **C** The 1989 CITES ban on poaching ended illegal ivory trafficking.
   - **D** Elephants are known to have good memories.

4. The exclamation mark at the end of the opening sentence of Text 2 expresses
   - **A** surprise.
   - **B** fear.
   - **C** strong feeling.
   - **D** dismay.

5. The author's attitude to ivory poaching is
   - **A** matter-of-fact.
   - **B** highly critical.
   - **C** approving.
   - **D** congratulatory.

6. How does the image of elephants' tusks add meaning to Text 2?

   ....

   ....

   ....

   ....

   ....

Get creative

7. Find out three facts about elephants not included in Text 1 (Unit 13A) or Text 2.

Answers and explanations on page 118

READING AND COMPREHENSION

Text 1

Brrr Brrrr. Brrr Brrrr.

Hi Auntie Di. It's Meg here.

Well, thank you. And you?

Today? Well, Mum and Dad took our whole family by train and then bus to see the sand-sculpting competition at Cottesloe Beach. The sculptures were absolutely astonishing! It felt like being in an enchanted world.

I think it's the detail. I've made plenty of sandcastles but it's so hard to make the sand do what you want it to do! But these sculptures had groups of people dressed in costumes that showed every wrinkle. Their faces had such realistic expressions you wanted to touch them to see if they were alive.

It was one that made me laugh. It had three parts—a dog, a human figure and a rock. Yes—that was my favourite. They looked so funny posed in the middle of the sand.

Oh really? Where did you see that one?

They have sand-sculpting competitions in Russia then? I'd just love to have seen the *Thumbelina* series.

Do they really—everywhere? Maybe one day then, when I go travelling, I'll visit all the places in the world that have sand-sculpting competitions. Especially the international ones because they sound really special.

That's a great idea. I'll google sand sculptures and see what I can find. Thanks Auntie Di.

Ok. See you soon then. Bye.

1 The sculpture that made Meg laugh had .... parts.
A one B two C three D four

2 Where had Meg just been?
A Russia B Thumbelina
C Perth D Cottesloe Beach

3 This text is one side of
A a radio programme.
B a telephone conversation.
C a live discussion.
D an imaginary conversation.

4 The sculpture Meg liked best
A had faces with realistic expressions.
B had costumes that showed wrinkles.
C was part of the *Thumbelina* series.
D was of a dog, a human and a rock.

5 Auntie Di
A has seen sand sculptures in Russia.
B knows the story of Thumbelina.
C has won a sand-sculpture competition.
D is someone Meg dislikes.

6 Is it easy to work out what Auntie Di says to Meg? Why or why not?

....

....

....

....

....

....

Answers and explanations on page 118

SPELLING

Rewrite the misspelt words in questions 1–4.

1 Look at that incredible sand scullpture!

2 They look so reallistic.

3 The plane leaves from the internashenal airport.

4 You could even see the wrinkels in her costume!

5 Write three words from the word family that includes **special**.

VOCABULARY

Circle the answers that have the nearest meaning to the underlined words in questions 6–7.

6 Did the whole family go?
- A completed
- B entire
- C full
- D total

7 They were posed like statues.
- A sitting
- B located
- C arranged
- D raised

8 Add a word from the text to the sentence.

I felt I was in a magical, ________ world.

9 Write a word from the text to match the meaning.

accurate and true to life

Circle the word that does **not** belong.

10
- A international
- B worldwide
- C global
- D national

11
- A usually
- B exceptionally
- C particularly
- D especially

GRAMMAR

12 Add a subjective adjective to the noun group.

Did you see the ________ sand sculpture?
- A Alice-in-Wonderland
- B miniature
- C spectacular
- D prize-winning

13 Name the tense of the underlined verbs.

I saved my pocket money and now I have enough to buy Mum a ticket.

14 Complete the sentence with an adverbial from the text that tells **how**.

We travelled ________ to Cottesloe.

15 Circle the relative pronoun in the sentence and underline the noun group to which it refers.

That sand sculpture, which made me laugh, won first prize.

PUNCTUATION

Rewrite the sentences correctly.

16 id have loved to see the *thumbelina* series

17 i think its in the detail dont you

18 ill google them now auntie di

Answers and explanations on pages 118–119

TEXTS IN CONTEXT

Text 2

Yesterday

I visited a sand-sculpture exhibition yesterday. There was a sculpture of Thumbelina, who had been captured by a rather nasty-looking toad. I'd heard of the Hans Christian Andersen fairytale, *Thumbelina*, but I'd never read it.

When I got home, I looked the story up on the internet. Poor Thumbelina! I learned she wasn't much bigger than a thumb and she found herself in danger as various animals tried to take over her life. Eventually, a lovelorn but unselfish swallow rescues her from her captors and flies her away to a country of flowers where she meets the King of the Flowers. At their wedding she is given the gift of gossamer wings and they live happily ever after.

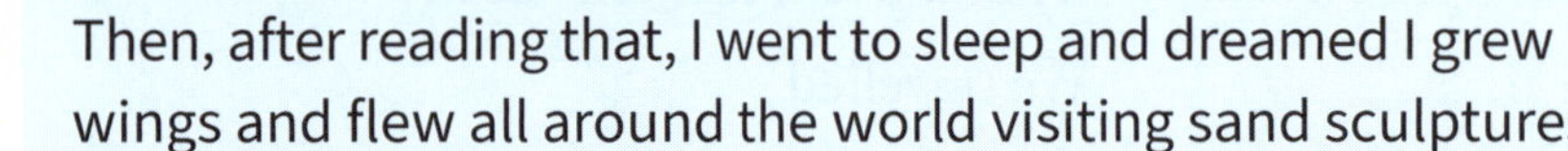

Then, after reading that, I went to sleep and dreamed I grew wings and flew all around the world visiting sand sculptures!

1. The purpose of Text 2 is to
   - **A** recount the previous day's activities.
   - **B** discuss sand sculptures.
   - **C** explain how to make a sand sculpture.
   - **D** describe what Thumbelina looked like.

2. In what sequence do the events occur?
   - **A** dreaming
   - **B** searching the internet
   - **C** visiting a sand-sculpture exhibition
   - **D** reading about Thumbelina

3. Which statement is **not** true? Both texts refer to
   - **A** sand-sculpture exhibitions.
   - **B** Thumbelina's rescue.
   - **C** searching the internet.
   - **D** visiting sand sculptures around the world.

4. Text 1 in Unit 14A and Text 2 have .... themes.
   - **A** identical **B** similar
   - **C** different **D** opposite

5. Meg's attitude to the art of sand sculpting in Text 1 (Unit 14A) is
   - **A** highly enthusiastic. **B** lukewarm.
   - **C** quite interested. **D** approving.

6. Does the summary of Thumbelina's story evoke an emotional response? Why or why not?

   ....

   ....

   ....

   ....

   ....

Get creative

7. Search for images of sand sculptures on the internet. Write down the name of a site you think has a good collection.

Answers and explanations on page 119

READING AND COMPREHENSION

Text 1

Advertising and children

Advertising, as an industry, did not really gain traction until the arrival of mass media. Print was a popular medium for advertisers during the 19th and early 20th centuries. The industry gained momentum with the advent of commercial radio in the 1920s and television in the 1950s. Since then, access to the internet has further expanded the industry's opportunities.

It took a long time for children to be targeted directly by advertisers. One of the earliest attempts at persuading children to want a product was an American television ad released in the 1950s. At that time, several toys that were to become classics were on the market: the frisbee, the Barbie doll and the hula hoop. In 1952 a television commercial was made for a toy called Mr Potato Head. It showed real children playing excitedly with, and talking about, their new toy. The original version of the toy consisted of facial features and body parts that could be stuck into a potato. Around 1955 other toy commercials were shown on the *Mickey Mouse Club* and the trend of appealing directly to children took hold. Today, targeting children directly is a multibillion-dollar industry.

Children are good targets for advertisers because they influence family spending and they spend money themselves. Furthermore they are very brand conscious—from the young child's early recognition of advertising signs and slogans to their more sophisticated understanding of which brands have peer acceptance.

However, there has been debate about the dangers involved in targeting young children in this way. Claims have been made that such advertisements often promote unhealthy choices and are a factor in causing childhood obesity; that they set up unrealistic goals and stereotypes; and that they turn children into consumer addicts.

1 What gave the advertising industry momentum in the 1920s?

A radio
B television
C print
D the internet

2 Which toy is not named a classic?

A the Barbie doll
B Mr Potato Head
C the hula hoop
D the frisbee

3 What changed after the success of ads on the *Mickey Mouse Club*?

A There were more ads on radio and television.
B Children bought toys for themselves.
C Brands began to change.
D Targeting children directly became a trend in advertising.

4 Advertisements 'turn children into consumer addicts' (line 22) means

A they encourage children to pester their parents.
B they force children to spend their money.
C they create the desire in children to want things.
D they offer children rewards for spending.

5 What does the word 'good' mean in line 14?

A well-behaved
B productive
C wise
D easy

6 Do you think advertisements targeting children should be banned? Why or why not?

....

....

Answers and explanations on page 119

SPELLING

Rewrite the misspelt words in questions 1–4.

1 Comercial radio was launched in the 1920s.

2 Our family isn't brand conshious.

3 They made some effective advertisments for toys.

4 That ad is full of gender stereotipes.

5 Write three words from the word family that includes **advertising**.

VOCABULARY

Circle the answers that have the nearest meaning to the underlined words in questions 6–7.

6 There are claims made both for and against the idea.

A answers B protests
C arguments D complaints

7 That could have a bad influence on children's behaviour.

A direction B result
C connection D effect

8 Add a word from the text to the sentence.

Which side do you take in the .... about the dangers of advertising?

9 Write words from the text to match the meaning.

technology that reaches a mass audience such as print, radio, television or the internet

Circle the word that does **not** belong.

10 A purchaser B buyer
C shopper D seller

11 A dissuade B advertise
C endorse D promote

GRAMMAR

12 Add a subjective adjective to the noun group.

My Barbie Doll has .... eyes.

A blue B plastic
C shiny D pretty

13 Name the tense of the underlined verb.

Do you think children's ads should be banned?

14 Complete the sentence with an adverbial from the text that tells **how**.

In the 1950s children were targeted ....

15 Circle the relative pronoun in the sentence and underline the noun group to which it refers.

The frisbee, which was popular in the 1950s, still sells well today.

PUNCTUATION

Rewrite the sentences correctly.

16 however television advertising was soon to increase

17 the frisbee hula hoop and barbie doll were fashionable then

18 have you ever watched the mickey mouse club

Answers and explanations on page 119

TEXTS IN CONTEXT

Text 2

THE GROOVY SMOOVY MAKER

Do these smoovys make your mouth water?

They can be yours in seconds. All you need is a Groovy Smoovy Maker. At the press of a button you'll be popular with everyone.

Groovy Smoovy Makers: available at good stores everywhere.

1. The purpose of Text 2 is to
   - **A** explain how to make groovy smoovys.
   - **B** describe what a Groovy Smoovy Maker can do.
   - **C** discuss the benefits of a Groovy Smoovy Maker.
   - **D** promote the sale of Groovy Smoovy Makers.

2. Text 2 is aimed at
   - **A** a general audience.
   - **B** males.
   - **C** females.
   - **D** children.

3. Text 1 in Unit 15A is .... advertising while Text 2 is ....
   - **A** full of/full of facts
   - **B** about an aspect of/an advertisement
   - **C** against/in favour
   - **D** in favour of/against

4. The author of Text 1 in Unit 15A .... the banning of ads directed at children.
   - **A** is clearly opposed to
   - **B** is highly supportive of
   - **C** does not express a view of their own about
   - **D** is in favour of

5. Which advertising techniques are evident in Text 2?
   - **A** appeal to envy
   - **B** repetition
   - **C** association with healthy eating
   - **D** exaggerated claims

6. Give a reason to support the view that advertising directly to children should **not** be banned.

   ....

   ....

   ....

   ....

   ....

   ....

Get creative

7. Invent a product and create an advertisement for its promotion.

Answers and explanations on page 119

Text 1

The history of spectacles

From far back in human history, people have found ways to improve their sight. It is claimed the Roman Emperor Nero watched the gladiator games through an emerald! There is also evidence that the Greeks filled glass bowls with water in order to magnify small print. In the 13th century, Italian monks crafted semi-shaped ground lenses which could be used as magnifying glasses.

These early glasses were soon made with two lenses riveted together. They could be held or worn on the face by pinching them tightly onto the nose. Various materials such as bone, wood or metal, and in later times wire or leather, were used to house the glass.

In the 1600s the rigid nose bridge appeared and shortly after that, frames—called temple frames—were made in one piece. You usually bought these from a pedlar (someone who travels from place to place selling small goods). In the 1800s rimmed spectacles and monocles came into vogue. The choice of lens was still a matter of trial and error.

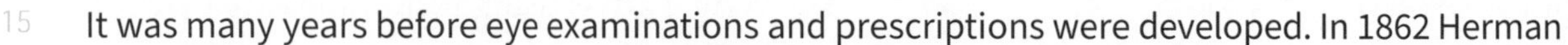

It was many years before eye examinations and prescriptions were developed. In 1862 Herman Snellen, a Dutch ophthalmologist, developed an eye chart which could be used to measure clarity of vision. This chart is still used today for eyesight tests.

In the early 20th century, spectacles gained their current form. They are now made from a variety of materials other than glass. Styles of glasses go in and out of fashion. In the last few decades Harry Potter, a character from a successful book and television series, has made wearing glasses very popular, particularly among children.

1 What nationality was the person who developed the eye chart?
- A English
- B German
- C Italian
- D Dutch

2 The word 'riveted' (line 6) means
- A joined.
- B completed.
- C hammered.
- D frozen.

3 Which is the most likely reason Nero put an emerald to his eye?
- A to make everything look green
- B to attract attention
- C to make it easier to see the gladiators
- D to show off his power

4 What is a monocle?
- A a popular type of spectacles
- B glasses that were only worn in the 1800s
- C a pair of lenses
- D a single lens used with one eye

5 What is an ophthalmologist?
- A an eye specialist
- B a glass blower
- C a doctor
- D a mechanic

6 In which order were these glasses used?
- A Harry Potter glasses
- B glasses with a rigid bridge
- C glasses with lens riveted together
- D glasses with temple frames

7 The picture adds .... the text.
- A a useful diagram for
- B a visual explanation of
- C a touch of humour to
- D an advertisement for

8 Why would high-tech plastics, rather than glass, be used to make spectacles now?

....

....

....

Answers and explanations on page 120

Text 2

Guess what?

Sal: Did you get anything for your birthday yesterday, Jimbo?

Jimbo: Yes! I got some faith, hope, love and luck.

Sal: What do you mean?

Jimbo: Well, you have to guess. My grandmother gave it to me. She said it took her two years to find the present.

Sal: I can't think of anything. Can you touch it? Or is it a magic lamp with a genie perhaps?

Jimbo: You can touch it. I've put it away between the pages of my diary. It's not a genie though.

Sal: What colour is it?

Jimbo: It's green.

Sal: Does it have four leaves?

Jimbo: You've got it! I found out that the statistical odds of finding a four-leaf clover the first time you look is ten thousand to one. And if you look for a five-leaf one, the odds become one million to one.

Sal: I didn't even know there *were* five-leaf clovers.

Jimbo: Are you doing anything later today? Shall we give it a try?

9 Text 2 is

- A a set of instructions.
- B a conversation.
- C a discussion.
- D an interview.

10 Which clue is the most useful to Sal?

- A My grandmother gave it to me. (line 5)
- B She said it took her two years to find the present. (line 6)
- C You can touch it. (line 8)
- D I've put it away between the pages of my diary. (line 8)

11 Jimbo's reaction to his grandmother's present was

- A disappointed and cross.
- B ecstatic and highly excited.
- C appreciative and interested.
- D anxious and concerned.

12 How do you think Sal would answer Jimbo's last question? (line 17)

Answers and explanations on page 120

Each sentence in questions 1–6 has one word that is incorrect. Write the correct spelling of each word in the boxes below.

1 She wasn't noticable in the crowd.

2 We acknowleged the traditional owners of the land.

3 The rhinoseros is a magnificent animal.

4 We are very priveledged to live here.

5 He thortlessly threw his empty cup into the bushland.

6 All my family loves walnuts but I loath them!

7 Which is a subjective adjective in this sentence?

Dad's delicious orange cake won first prize at the local show.

A delicious B orange
C first D local

8 Which word adds meaning to a noun in this sentence?

The lazy fox lay sleeping soundly in the sun.

A lazy B sleeping
C soundly D the

9 In which sentence is **shape** used as a noun?

A I woke up and saw a strange shape standing in front of me.
B I plan to shape the dough into a loaf of bread.
C My ice cream was made in the shape of a tower.
D Dad told me he was in pretty good shape!

10 Add the modal verb that expresses the **most** certainty in this sentence.

You .... help your sister with her homework.

A could B will C must D should

11 Which verb group correctly completes the sentence?

I .... to see her for over a year now.

A hasn't been B isn't going
C wasn't going D haven't been

12 Circle the word group that tells **how** the elephant was looked after.

The elephant, who was limping badly, was soon looked after by his mother.

13 Which **two** phrases could correctly complete the sentence?

We are leaving .... for the airport.

A at 6 am
B as quickly as we could
C to fly to an island
D very early tomorrow

14 Which word is the subject of this sentence?

During afternoon tea, Mary revealed a family secret.

A tea B Mary C revealed D family

15 Why is there an apostrophe in this sentence?

It's my birthday party tomorrow.

A to mark a missing letter
B to show ownership
C to mark a plural
D to avoid ambiguity

16 Which sentence is **not** punctuated correctly?

A Tigers live in tropical forests, mangrove swamps, grasslands and savannahs.
B The brushtail possum is mostly nocturnal (more active at night).
C The echidna and the platypus are the only living mammals, who lay eggs.
D Foxes have upright ears, a pointed, slightly upturned snout and a bushy tail.

Answers and explanations on page 120

READING AND COMPREHENSION

Text 1

My favourite book

My favourite book changes all the time! But for quite a long time now it's been *The Word Spy*, written by Ursula Dubosarsky and illustrated by Tohby Riddle. It's all about words and their secrets—you'd never guess how intriguing and interesting these turn out to be!

Something I love about the book is the way the Word Spy talks directly to me and treats me as one of her spies. This means I can learn the secrets known by the Word Spy but I can also find out things by doing some spying myself.

After a while, you think of the Word Spy as a friend you like spending time with. She talks in such a friendly way to the reader, almost as if she knows how you think and feel. She makes up amusing, nonsensical sentences to illustrate her comments and, before you know it, you understand lots of things you didn't before.

I loved the chapter on punctuation which begins with the word CANYOUREADTHISSENTENCE. I had thought the rules about punctuation were somehow always there, fixed in cement, but you learn that once upon a time only capital letters were used, there were no spaces between words and you could spell words however you liked. I also liked learning what names other countries use for quotation marks: 'goose feet' in Icelandic; 'fingernail marks' in Turkish; and 'cats' claws' in Hungarian.

There is even a hidden secret message in the book that involves the reader in deciphering many different codes. By the end of the book you have become an expert codebreaker! I won't tell you what the secret message is because I don't want to spoil the fun for you.

by Oliver

1 Who wrote *The Word Spy*?
- A Oliver
- B Tohby Riddle
- C Ursula Dubosarsky
- D The Word Spy

2 *The Word Spy* is about
- A words and their secrets.
- B punctuation.
- C spelling.
- D different languages.

3 Oliver thinks reading *The Word Spy* has
- A made him an expert in spying.
- B changed his thoughts about the 'rules' of language.
- C made him better at grammar.
- D turned him into a language cop.

4 What does the word 'illustrate' (line 10) mean?
- A serve as examples for
- B decorate
- C draw pictures of
- D adorn

5 Does Oliver's review make you want to read the book? Why or why not?

....

....

6 What is the main reason *The Word Spy* is a favourite for Oliver?

....

....

Answers and explanations on page 120

SPELLING

Rewrite the misspelt words in questions 1–4.

1 There is so much intriging information.

2 She enjoys making up nonnsensical sentences.

3 I thought the rules were fixed in cemeant!

4 Are you good at desiphering codes?

5 Write three words from the word family that includes **secret**.

VOCABULARY

Circle the answers that have the nearest meaning to the underlined words in questions 6–7.

6 I'm never sure when to use quotation marks.
A spoken B speech
C saying D punctuation

7 Do you think words are intriguing?
A absorbing B unusual
C worrying D enthralling

8 Add a word from the text to the sentence.
Did you know that once upon a time people only used ______ letters.

9 Write a word from the text to match the meaning.
having no meaning; making no sense

Circle the word that does **not** belong.

10 A rules B regulations
C laws D suggestions

11 A decode B decipher
C guess D solve

GRAMMAR

12 Circle the noun group that includes an adjectival phrase.
When you reach the end of the book you'll be a codebreaker!

13 Add an auxiliary (helping) verb to complete the sentence.
I ______ just read *The Return of the Word Spy*.

14 Complete the sentence with a modal adverb from the text.
I thought those rules might ______ stay in place for ever!

15 Which word connects the subordinate clause to the main clause?
Ursula Dubosarsky is a writer who has many novels to her name.
A writer B who
C many D to

PUNCTUATION

Rewrite the sentences correctly.

16 she makes up nonsensical amusing sentences

17 quotation marks are called cats claws in hungarian

18 in no time at all youll find youre an expert

Answers and explanations on page 120

TEXTS IN CONTEXT

Text 2

punctuation

punctuation is unnecessary said pandora looking her teacher in the eye she gazed at Adrian for admiration but got none he was looking at someone else she organised a meeting to ban punctuation adrian will you be chairman she asked no I cant come on Monday he said well then another day she pleaded no I like punctuation he replied he is a brain thought pandora reverently otherwise he wouldn't like punctuation the meeting was cancelled one day someone passed her a note I love you Adrian it said somebody loves him she thought she jumbled up the note jealously after school he said why did you crumple up my note she said because I was jealous he said but it was for you it said I love you Adrian oh she said I thought it said I love you Adrian no he said

'I like punctuation,' she said.

1 Text 2 is a
- **A** poem.
- **B** play.
- **C** narrative.
- **D** recount.

2 Text 1 in Unit 16A is a
- **A** review.
- **B** discussion.
- **C** letter.
- **D** reminiscence.

3 Text 2 makes it clear that
- **A** there's no point to punctuation.
- **B** punctuation gets in the way of meaning.
- **C** punctuation can change meaning.
- **D** meaning is independent of punctuation.

4 Why is the last line of Text 2 in a paragraph by itself? Choose **all** that apply.
- **A** to mark a change in the writing
- **B** to show Pandora is good at punctuation
- **C** to add a happy ending
- **D** to add emphasis and humour

5 Text 1 in Unit 16A and Text 2 are concerned, in different ways, with
- **A** how language works.
- **B** how punctuation adds meaning.
- **C** how to be a spy.
- **D** how to play word games.

6 Does Text 2 convince you of the value of punctuation?

....

....

....

....

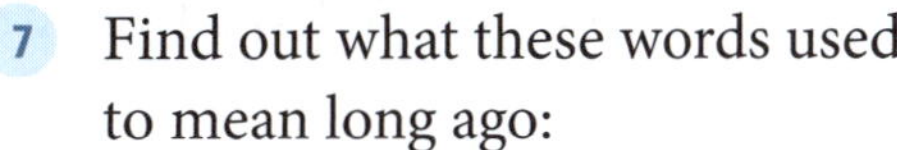

7 Find out what these words used to mean long ago:

let awful terrific

Answers and explanations on pages 120–121

 Text 1

From the newsroom

It's well known that those who've never visited Australia, particularly Americans, often view Down Under as a place where kangaroos hop along its main streets. How could they possibly think that about our elegant, modern, thriving cities?

Well, Sydney motorists on their way to work at around 5 am last week must have thought they were seeing things. For right there, as you can see on your screens, hopping along beside them on the bridge, was a male adult swamp wallaby! He avoided all traffic regulations and took himself lane hopping. After he crossed from lane one, where he was first sighted, to lane eight, on the opposite side of the bridge, he set off down the Cahill Expressway and on to the Macquarie Street exit. Yes: someone was certainly hopping mad today! Police were finally able to catch him near the Conservatorium of Music.

'It was a first for all of us,' said a policeman who arrived at the scene to rescue the wallaby. 'None of us had ever seen a wallaby crossing the Harbour Bridge before! And to add to the excitement, we were helped to capture him by no less than a former captain of the Wallabies, Nick Farr-Jones, who was on his way to work.' After caring for the wallaby as best they could, he was transported by the police to Taronga Zoo where he was admitted to the Taronga Wildlife Hospital. A senior veterinarian took over his care.

The wallaby, nicknamed Skippy, a name familiar to Australians from the early days of television, is reported to be on the mend. When he fully recovers from the stress of his adventure, the plan is to release him in the Ku-ring-gai Chase National Park.

LATE NEWS: A report just in from Adelaide states that a kangaroo has been sighted hopping down Rundle St. Perhaps those foreigners know something we don't!

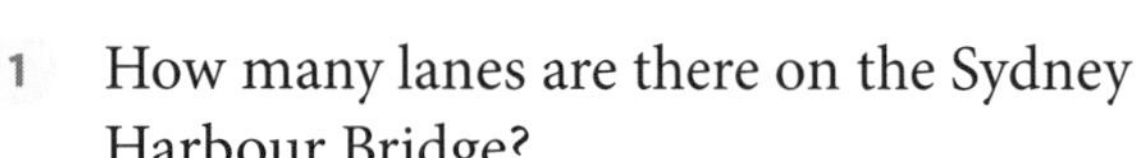

1 How many lanes are there on the Sydney Harbour Bridge?
- A two
- B four
- C six
- D eight

2 Where was the wallaby to be released?
- A Sydney Harbour Bridge
- B Ku-ring-gai Chase National Park
- C Taronga Zoo
- D Taronga Wildlife Hospital

3 Who was 'hopping mad' (line 10)?
- A commuters, who were angry to have their journey interrupted
- B the wallaby, who engaged in a frenzy of hopping
- C the traffic police because the wallaby was breaking their rules
- D Nick Farr-Jones because he had to catch the wallaby

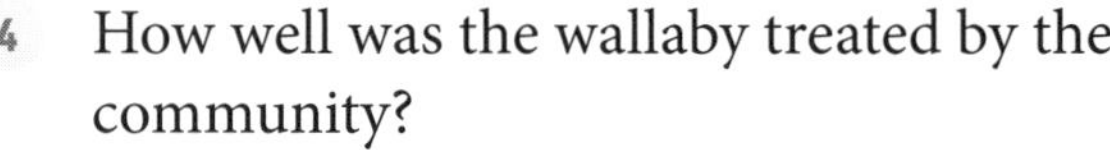

4 How well was the wallaby treated by the community?
- A exceptionally well
- B quite well
- C rather carelessly
- D rather thoughtlessly

5 Who are the 'foreigners' referred to in line 24?
- A people who live in Adelaide
- B those who've never visited Australia
- C Americans
- D visitors to Australia

6 Is this news report better suited to television or radio?

....

....

Answers and explanations on page 121

SPELLING

Rewrite the misspelt words in questions 1–4.

1 There's a wallabie on our bridge!

2 It left the expressway and entered Maquarry Street.

3 Skippy was looked at by a vetinarian.

4 I don't like my Nikname.

5 Write three words from the word family that includes **sighted**.

VOCABULARY

Circle the answers that have the nearest meaning to the underlined words in questions 6–7.

6 When I travel to America, I'm legally described as a foreigner.
A an alien B a visitor
C an outsider D a native

7 Is Skippy a name that is familiar to you?
A remarkable B unknown
C related D recognisable

8 Add a word from the text to the sentence.

The police ______ Skippy in their van to the zoo.

9 Write a word from the text to match the meaning.

laws, rules or other orders prescribed by authority, especially to regulate conduct

Circle the word that does **not** belong.

10 A stylish B elegant
C unsophisticated D smart

11 A recover B get well
C convalesce D get back

GRAMMAR

12 Circle the noun group that includes an adjectival phrase.

The motorists on their way to work thought they were seeing things!

13 Add an auxiliary (helping) verb to complete the sentence.

______ they able to catch the wallaby without hurting him?

14 Complete the sentence with a modal adverb from the text.

How can you ______ think that?

15 Which word connects the subordinate clause to the main clause?

Skippy was a bush kangaroo who had lots of adventures.

A bush B kangaroo
C who D lots

PUNCTUATION

Rewrite the sentences correctly.

16 we live in elegant modern cities

17 a male swamp wallaby hopped along the sydney harbour bridge

18 my uncle nicknamed Speed can run very quickly

Answers and explanations on page 121

 **Text 2**

Fact file: swamp wallabies

Swamp wallabies (*Wallabia bicolor*)

1 are small marsupials
2 are native to Australia and live mainly on the Eastern coast
3 have dark brown to black back fur, yellow to reddish orange belly fur and a light yellow to brownish cheek stripe
4 get their name from areas they inhabit (Maybe they have a swampy smell!)
5 shelter in the thick undergrowth of forests, woodlands and marshes
6 are herbivores
7 have an unusual gait for a wallaby, carrying their head low with the tail held straight
8 are mainly solitary, nocturnal animals.

1 Text 2 is
- **A** an advertisement for the preservation of wallabies.
- **B** a discussion of the features of *Wallabia bicolor.*
- **C** a description of what a swamp wallaby looks like.
- **D** a list of facts about *Wallabia bicolor.*

2 Text 1 in Unit 17A is
- **A** a recount about events in sequence.
- **B** a summary of a response to an event.
- **C** a report of facts about a particular animal.
- **D** a procedure about how to do something.

3 The LATE NEWS at the end of Text 1 in Unit 17A is
- **A** important national news.
- **B** important global news.
- **C** quite serious.
- **D** amusingly ironic.

4 Why are brackets used in Text 2 number 4?
- **A** to draw attention to what is said
- **B** to give a fuller explanation
- **C** to explain an idea
- **D** to separate what may be an opinion from the facts

5 The tone of Text 1 (Unit 17A) is .... whereas that of Text 2 is ....
- **A** witty/humorous
- **B** lighthearted/matter of fact
- **C** anxious/confident
- **D** hypocritical/self-important

6 How comprehensive is the information provided in Text 2?

....

....

Get creative

7 Write a news report about an animal doing something unusual.

Answers and explanations on page 121

READING AND COMPREHENSION

Text 1

Come to Arnhem Land

Arnhem Land

Looking for somewhere different? About 500 km from Darwin, in the north-eastern corner of the Northern Territory, there is a truly special part of Australia that will tick all your boxes. Its name? Arnhem Land. Indigenous people have lived here for tens of thousands of years. Today it has a small population of around 16 000 people, most of whom are Aboriginal.

Looking for distinctive scenery? Arnhem Land, named after the ship of a captain of the Dutch East India Company who sailed into the Gulf of Carpentaria in 1623, includes the world-famous Kakadu National Park. It gained World Heritage listing in the 1990s and its vast area of unspoilt wilderness includes stone country with rugged escarpments and magnificent ancient rainforests. The natural features of Arnhem Land—ranging from rivers, estuaries, tidal flats and floodplains to pristine shores, rugged coastlines and remote islands—make it a winner in anybody's book.

Looking for a unique history and culture? Doubtless you won't want to miss the many examples of rock paintings. A recent find near the northern reaches of the Katherine River was described as 'one of the biggest Aboriginal art galleries in Australia'. At the Black Point Cultural Centre you'll find displays of Aboriginal, Macassan and European histories of the area. You can also meet the Aboriginal communities of Yirrkala or Gunbalanya, who are internationally famous for their bark paintings.

Look no further! Can't wait? For details of gaining a permit, itineraries and costs, contact **Arnhem Land Tours** today.

1 How long have Indigenous people lived in Arnhem Land?
- A 16 000 years
- B since 1623
- C tens of thousands of years
- D since the 1990s

2 Where could you see a display of the Macassan history of the area?
- A beside the Katherine River
- B at the Black Point Cultural Centre
- C at the Dutch East India Company
- D at the Yirrkala Community Centre

3 Which words would you click on to ask more about an Arnhem Land Tour?
- A HOME
- B PLACES TO VISIT
- C MAPS
- D CONTACT US

4 Why do the first three paragraphs begin with a question? Choose **all** that apply.
- A to promote Arnhem Land Tours
- B to create a pattern that is memorable
- C to separate the paragraphs
- D to make the information given look impressive

5 What is the emphasis of this text?
- A the unique, engaging experiences on offer
- B the many virtues of the tour company
- C the extraordinary value for money offered
- D the international fame of the place

6 How well does the writer justify the view that Arnhem Land is unusual?

Answers and explanations on page 121

SPELLING

Rewrite the misspelt words in questions 1–4.

1 Many Indidgenous people live in Arnhem Land. ....

2 It's beautiful natural features are spectacular.

....

3 Kakadu has World Heritidge status.

....

4 The anshient forests are truly beautiful.

....

5 Write three words from the word family that includes **special**.

....

....

VOCABULARY

Circle the answers that have the nearest meaning to the underlined words in questions 6–7.

6 Unspoilt wilderness covers a vast area.

A Unnatural B Genuine
C Real D Natural

7 You need a permit to visit.

A visa B passport
C authorisation D ticket

8 Add a word from the text to the sentence.

Kakadu National Park is on the World .... list.

9 Write a word from the text to match the meaning.

a travel document recording a route or journey ....

Circle the word that does **not** belong.

10 A citizens B household
C inhabitants D population

11 A rugged B rough
C craggy D wrinkled

GRAMMAR

12 Circle the noun group that includes an adjectival phrase.

Did you know the bark paintings of Yirrkala are famous?

13 Add an auxiliary (helping) verb to complete the sentence.

.... you ever visited Kakadu?

14 Complete the sentence with a modal adverb from the text.

.... you'll ring that travel agent as soon as possible.

15 Which word connects the subordinate clause to the main clause?

We are leaving on a jet plane when Gran has bought our tickets.

A on
B when
C has
D bought

PUNCTUATION

Rewrite the sentences correctly.

16 looking for somewhere different

....

....

17 they range from rivers estuaries and floodplains to unspoilt shores

....

....

18 were going to look no further

....

....

Answers and explanations on pages 121–122

TEXTS IN CONTEXT

Text 2

1. The main purpose of this text is to
   - A explain how to hold your soap.
   - B reveal what the soap looks like unwrapped.
   - C persuade people to buy Pears' soap.
   - D describe the importance of soap.
2. Text 1 in Unit 18A is
   - A a review.
   - B an advertisement.
   - C a discussion.
   - D an explanation.
3. Choose **all** that apply. Text 1 in Unit 18A aims to attract people who are
   - A keen on physical activity.
   - B interested in history and culture.
   - C interested in the natural world.
   - D animal lovers.
4. Text 2 aims to associate Pears' soap with
   - A busy working women.
   - B respectable, elegant females.
   - C active young mothers.
   - D weary mothers.
5. Which statement is **not** true? Text 1 in Unit 18A and Text 2
   - A make particular words bold for emphasis.
   - B include emotive language to promote their products.
   - C rely strongly on a visual image to be persuasive.
   - D use capital letters to draw attention to particular words.
6. Which is the more effective text: Text 1 in Unit 18A or Text 2? Explain your answer.

....

....

....

....

....

....

....

....

....

Get creative

7. Find out what wildlife you could see on a visit to Arnhem Land.

Answers and explanations on page 122

READING AND COMPREHENSION

 Text 1

Elizabeth Batts Cook (1742–1835)

Elizabeth Batts was born in 1742 in Essex, England. Her father, an innkeeper, died a few months after she was born. Very little is known of Elizabeth's early life.

On 21 December 1762, Elizabeth married James Cook (1728–99) and they set up home in London's East End near the Docks. Six years after their marriage, James was chosen to take command of the *Endeavour*, a role which led to his fame as a navigator and explorer. The Cooks had six children. Elizabeth outlived both her husband and all her children.

Elizabeth was a very talented embroiderer and used her skills to honour her husband's achievements. An embroidered map sampler*, attributed to her and now held in the Australian National Maritime Museum collection, outlines her husband's three voyages to the Pacific. The map depicts various continents and countries; the equator; the tropics of Cancer and Capricorn; the Pacific, Atlantic and Southern oceans; and lines of latitude and longitude. Tiny stitches trace each of his voyages on the map.

At the time James Cook was speared to death in the Sandwich Islands, Hawaii, Elizabeth was in the process of embroidering a vest for him to wear at court after his return. The vest, made with tapa cloth James had brought back from his second voyage, is now in its unfinished state in the Mitchell Library, Sydney, Australia.

The sailors on Cook's last ship, the HMS *Resolution*, presented Elizabeth with a carved 'ditty-box'**, in which she kept a tiny painting of Cook's death and a lock of his hair. Before she died she destroyed her husband's letters, probably because she wanted to keep their personal relationship private.

*Learning to sew samplers of this kind was a popular educational tool.
**a sailor's box for personal belongings

1 In which year did Elizabeth's husband die?
A 1728 B 1742 C 1762 D 1799

2 Who gave Elizabeth a 'ditty-box'?
A her father
B her husband
C sailors from HMS *Resolution*
D staff at the Mitchell Library

3 Why would an 'unfinished' (line 17) vest be kept?
A to have a memento of an important moment in history
B to preserve cloth and silks which were valuable
C to avoid wasting public money
D to provide proof that Cook was expected at court

4 That the sampler is 'attributed' (line 11) to Elizabeth means
A someone else made it.
B she almost certainly made it.
C she might have made it.
D she might have made some of it.

5 How would you describe Elizabeth's attitude to her husband?
A friendly and easygoing
B disappointed and upset
C annoyed and critical
D devoted and admiring

6 How would you sum up the life of Elizabeth Cook?

Answers and explanations on page 122

SPELLING

Rewrite the misspelt words in questions 1–4.

1 Have you visited the Marritime Museum?

2 Can you guess which continennts were included?

3 It was a magnificently embroydered sampler.

4 He sailed to Australia on the Endevour.

5 Write three words from the word family that includes **fame**.

VOCABULARY

Circle the answers that have the nearest meaning to the underlined words in questions 6–7.

6 He took command of the ship in 1768.
A direction B charge
C government D oversight

7 The vest remained unfinished.
A incomplete B adorned
C amateurish D bare

8 Add a word from the text to the sentence.

Lines of latitude and ______ were included.

9 Write a word from the text to match the meaning.

a piece of cloth embroidered with various stitches to show skill in needlework

Circle the word that does **not** belong.

10 A speared B impaled
C stabbed D inserted

11 A talented B capable
C skilled D accomplished

GRAMMAR

12 Circle the noun group that includes an adjectival phrase.

Samplers of this kind were a popular educational tool.

13 Add an auxiliary (helping) verb to complete the sentence.

______ you like to see Elizabeth Cook's needlework?

14 Complete the sentence with a modal adverb from the text.

I think that she ______ had good reason to burn the letters.

15 Which word connects the subordinate clause to the main clause?

Captain Cook was on his way home when he was felled by a spear.

A was B his
C home D when

PUNCTUATION

Rewrite the sentences correctly.

16 james cook 1728–99 commanded the *endeavour*

17 the cooks had six children

18 before she died elizabeth destroyed her husbands letters

Answers and explanations on page 122

TEXTS IN CONTEXT

Text 2

Mrs Macquarie's Chair

Mrs Elizabeth Macquarie, a Scottish-born woman, was the wife of Lachlan Macquarie. They sailed together to Australia when he came to take up the position of Governor of New South Wales in 1810. To honour his wife and her work, Governor Macquarie had convicts carve a chair out of sandstone on a pensinsula in Sydney Harbour. This was an area where Elizabeth liked to walk or sit and watch the ships arrive from Great Britain.

Above the Chair is an inscription referring to Mrs Macquarie's Road, which originally ran from Government House to Mrs Macquarie's Point. Mrs Macquarie's Chair remains a popular tourist attraction today.

1 The main purpose of Text 2 is to
- **A** recount events.
- **B** describe a historical artefact.
- **C** explain a process.
- **D** promote an attitude.

2 Text 1 in Unit 19A is
- **A** a recount.
- **B** an exposition.
- **C** an information report.
- **D** a discussion.

3 Both Text 1 in Unit 19A and Text 2
- **A** are biographies.
- **B** include biographical information.
- **C** show strong bias.
- **D** dramatise events.

4 Which answer best describes the structure of Text 1 in Unit 19A?
- **A** point of view with supporting reasons
- **B** orientation, complication, resolution
- **C** introduction, series of events in time sequence
- **D** general statement, statements about the topic, conclusion

5 Which answer best describes the structure of Text 2?
- **A** a sequence of arguments and evidence
- **B** background information, description of features, final comment
- **C** point of view with supporting reasons
- **D** orientation, complication, resolution

6 What might Elizabeth Cook and Elizabeth Macquarie have talked about if they'd met?

....

....

....

7 Find out what Elizabeth Macquarie did for the colony when she was in New South Wales between 1810 and 1821.

Answers and explanations on pages 122–123

READING AND COMPREHENSION

Text 1

From *The Call of the Wild*

Chapter 1. Into the Primitive

Buck did not read the newspapers or he would have known that trouble was brewing, not alone for himself, but for every tide-water dog, strong of muscle and with warm, long hair, from Puget Sound to San Diego. Because men, groping in the Arctic darkness, had found a yellow metal, and because steamship and transportation companies were booming the find, thousands of men were rushing into the Northland. These men wanted dogs and the dogs they wanted were heavy dogs, with strong muscles by which to toil, and furry coats to protect them from the frost.

Buck lived at a big house in the sun-kissed Santa Clara Valley. Judge Miller's place, it was called. It stood back from the road, half hidden among the trees, through which glimpses could be caught of the wide cool veranda that ran around its four sides.

…

And over this great demesne Buck ruled.

…

But Buck was neither house-dog nor kennel-dog. The whole realm was his. He plunged into the swimming tank or went hunting with the Judge's sons; he escorted Mollie and Alice, the Judge's daughters, on long twilight or early morning rambles; on wintry nights he lay at the Judge's feet before the roaring library fire; he carried the Judge's grandsons on his back, or rolled them in the grass, and guarded their footsteps through wild adventures down to the fountain in the stable yard, and even beyond, where the paddocks were, and the berry patches. Among the terriers he stalked imperiously, and Toots and Ysabel he utterly ignored, for he was king,—king over all creeping, crawling, flying things of Judge Miller's place, humans included.

Extract from *The Call of the Wild* by Jack London, 1903 (www.gutenberg.org/files/215/215-h/215-h.htm)

1 Who were Mollie and Alice?
- A Judge Miller's daughters
- B two terriers
- C Buck's childhood friends
- D Toots and Ysabel's cousins

2 Buck lived in a big house in
- A the Northland.
- B San Diego.
- C Puget Sound.
- D the Santa Clara Valley.

3 Why didn't Buck read the newspapers?
- A They weren't delivered to Judge Miller's place.
- B Dogs can't read.
- C Judge Miller had forbidden it.
- D He didn't have the time.

4 Why was trouble brewing for certain types of dogs?
- A They were strong and hairy.
- B Men needed their fur.
- C Men needed their help in finding gold in the Arctic.
- D They would be taken to protect them from the frost.

5 Which is most likely? Buck will
- A stay at Judge Miller's forever.
- B be taken North by the men who desperately want dogs.
- C be overpowered by the terriers.
- D go to live with Judge Miller's grandchildren.

6 Why is Buck described as a 'king' (line 20)?

....

....

Answers and explanations on page 123

SPELLING

Rewrite the misspelt words in questions 1–4.

1 They made an amazing discovery in the Artic.

2 The dogs they wanted would have strong mussels.

3 He stalked impeeriously past them.

4 He ignawed Toots, the Japanese pug.

5 Write three words from the word family that includes **humans**.

VOCABULARY

Circle the answers that have the nearest meaning to the underlined words in questions 6–7.

6 I wore my warm coat as it was such a wintry day.
A desolate B chilly
C unhappy D cheerless

7 Buck guarded the Judge's grandsons from harm.
A protected B watched
C defended D covered

8 Add a word from the text to the sentence.
It's not surprising that trouble was .

9 Write a word from the text to match the meaning.
an early state of human development

Circle the word that does **not** belong.

10 A ignored B lost
C avoided D evaded

11 A wild B untamed
C savage D native

GRAMMAR

12 Circle the noun group that includes an adjectival phrase.
The dogs with strong muscles and furry coats were much in demand.

13 Add an auxiliary (helping) verb to complete the sentence.
He'd heard thousands of men rushing into the Northland.

14 Complete the sentence with a modal adverb from the text.
He ignored the other dogs.

15 Which word connects the subordinate clause to the main clause?
Men rushed to the Northlands where they hoped to find gold.
A Northlands B where
C they D hoped

PUNCTUATION

Rewrite the sentences correctly.

16 the house was in the sunkissed santa clara valley

17 buck hunted with the judges sons

18 all creeping crawling flying things were under his rule

Answers and explanations on page 123

TEXTS IN CONTEXT

 Text 2

Dogs

Did you know? Dogs:

- have a sense of smell that is way better than a human's. They have between 225 to 300 million olfactory receptors in their noses, whereas humans have between five to six million
- have excellent hearing. They have muscles in their ears which allow them to move their ears both together or one at a time
- are good at finding their way home without a map. Some are known to have travelled vast distances to reach their homes
- do a variety of valuable jobs for humans. They can be trained to herd animals, to pull sleds and to act as guide dogs or sniffer dogs to identify bombs or drugs.

1 What is the purpose of Text 2?
- **A** to tell a story from a dog's point of view
- **B** to recount a series of events
- **C** to give some less well-known information about dogs
- **D** to describe dogs and explain what they do

2 Text 1 in Unit 20A is an extract from
- **A** a science-fiction novel.
- **B** an adventure story.
- **C** a journal.
- **D** a romance.

3 The second sentence of every dot point in Text 2
- **A** makes a new claim.
- **B** adds scientific evidence.
- **C** compares dogs with humans.
- **D** expands on what is said in the first sentence.

4 Text 1 in Unit 20A
- **A** is told from Buck's point of view.
- **B** is told from a narrator's point of view.
- **C** is a first-person narrative.
- **D** is told from Judge Miller's point of view.

5 How does the picture relate to the words of Text 2?

....

....

....

6 How does the title of Text 1 in Unit 20A relate to the extract from Chapter One?

....

....

....

....

Get creative

7 Use the internet to look at other covers for *Call of the Wild* by Jack London. Sketch a rough copy of the cover you think best suits the title of the novel.

Answers and explanations on page 123

READING AND COMPREHENSION

Text 1

Women's suffrage

❶ Good morning Ms Wild and Year 5.

❷ Suffrage is the right to vote in elections. Women's suffrage—you guessed it—is the right of women to vote in elections.

❸ I, Millie Brown, began my research into women's suffrage knowing almost nothing about it. I'd heard of Emmeline Pankhurst and the suffragettes in Britain and I knew that their continued political pressure on the government led to their getting the vote for women, though I didn't know when that happened. I also knew nothing about women's suffrage in Australia. When did they get the vote, I wondered? Presumably it was well after British women and I guessed it was probably long after American women. Did I have a lot to learn!

❹ The first colony in Australia to win the right to vote for women was South Australia, where in 1894 women could both vote and stand for election. Western Australia added voting rights in 1899. When the colonies federated in 1901, these rights continued and in 1902 the Commonwealth Parliament enabled all women to vote and stand for election for the Federal Parliament. State Parliaments followed over the next few years.

❺ Of course, this radical change didn't just happen. It was the result of long, hard campaigning by Temperance and Christian groups, women's suffrage societies and dedicated individuals. And yes, we had our own heroine suffragettes such as Mary Lee (South Australia) and Vida Goldstein (Victoria), along with many others, who achieved their goal well *before* Emmeline Pankhurst and her fellow suffragettes. Get that!

❻ So where did we come in the order of countries granting women the vote? In date order there was: New Zealand, 1893; Australia, 1902; USA, 1920; United Kingdom, 1928; and China and Japan, 1948. Of course, it was all much more complicated than these figures suggest but I'll save that story for next time.

1 What did Millie know when she began her research?
- A a great deal
- B a fair amount
- C a few things
- D almost nothing

2 What did Millie wonder (line 10)?
- A when Australian women got the vote
- B if Emmeline Pankhurst entered parliament
- C why American women got the vote
- D if she needed to do more research

3 What particularly surprised Millie? Choose **all** that apply.
- A that South Australia was the first colony to give women the vote
- B that New Zealand was the first country to give women the vote
- C that Australia had its own heroine suffragettes
- D that Australian women earned voting rights before Britain

4 Millie finds her topic
- A boring.
- B intriguing.
- C far too complicated.
- D dry and uninteresting.

5 How would you describe Millie's manner in delivering her speech?
- A timid
- B confident
- C conceited
- D nervous

6 If you were to judge Millie's speech in a competition would you rate it excellent, good, fair or poor? Explain.

....

....

....

....

Answers and explanations on page 123

SPELLING

Rewrite the misspelt words in questions 1–4.

1 Vida Goldstein was an Australian sufferagette. ……………

2 It was passed through the Parliment.

……………

3 They campained long and hard.

……………

4 The colonies phederated in 1901.

……………

5 Write three words from the word family that includes **heroine**.

……………

VOCABULARY

Circle the answers that have the nearest meaning to the underlined words in questions 6–7.

6 They were dedicated to their cause.

A disloyal B zealous
C devoted D disposed towards

7 Was Australia first in the order of countries giving women suffrage?

A command B sequence
C classification D distribution

8 Add a word from the text to the sentence.

It sounds simple but it is rather more …………… than it seems.

9 Write a word from the text to match the meaning.

extreme, especially as regards change from accepted or traditional forms

……………

Circle the word that does **not** belong.

10 A presumably B improbably
C doubtless D probably

11 A cause B product
C result D outcome

GRAMMAR

12 Circle the noun group that includes an adjectival phrase.

When I began my research into women's suffrage I knew very little.

13 Add an auxiliary (helping) verb to complete the sentence.

Where …………… you think we would come in the list of countries?

14 Complete the sentence with a modal adverb from the text.

I guessed that American women …………… got the vote before Australian women.

15 Which word connects the subordinate clause to the main clause?

I was really surprised because you kept that secret for such a long time.

A because B you
C secret D for

PUNCTUATION

Rewrite the sentences correctly.

16 did i have a lot to learn

……………

……………

17 of course there was plenty still to be done

……………

……………

18 womens suffrage was achieved slowly

……………

……………

Answers and explanations on pages 123–124

Text 2

Where were you born?

Our class did a survey to find out where we were born. Here are the results.

Country	Number born there	Country	Number born there
Australia	14	China	4
New Zealand	1	Israel	2
Indonesia	1	United Kingdom	3
Malaysia	1	USA	1
Japan	2	Germany	1

Conclusion: Just under half the class was born in Australia.

1 The main purpose of Text 2 is to
- **A** show the results of a survey.
- **B** ask students where they were born.
- **C** list the countries children come from.
- **D** compare the places where children were born.

2 The main purpose of Text 1 in Unit 21A is to
- **A** amuse an audience.
- **B** present an argument.
- **C** present information about a topic.
- **D** explain why events occurred.

3 Which question **cannot** be answered by using information from the table?
- **A** What gender are the Australian students?
- **B** Which country, other than Australia, had the most students born there?
- **C** How many students are in the class?
- **D** How many students were not born in Australia?

4 The language of Text 1 in Unit 21A is made up of
- **A** a mixture of slang and colloquial language.
- **B** formal language throughout.
- **C** a mixture of formal and colloquial language.
- **D** informal language throughout.

5 Text 1 in Unit 21A and Text 2 are
- **A** impersonal.
- **B** politically biased.
- **C** highly imaginative.
- **D** research based.

6 Match the paragraphs in Text 1 (Unit 21A) to the correct summary.

Paragraph 3 [ ]

Paragraph 4 [ ]

Paragraph 5 [ ]

Paragraph 6 [ ]

- **A** how women's suffrage was brought about in Australia
- **B** Millie's confession of what she doesn't know about the topic
- **C** the order in which countries achieved women's suffrage, with a caution
- **D** a brief overview of when women's suffrage began in Australia

Get creative

7 Survey a group of your classmates or family members to find out where they were born. Present your findings in a table.

Answers and explanations on page 124

READING AND COMPREHENSION

Text 1

Our research project

Dear Uncle Bill

As you are an ornithologist, I thought you'd be interested to hear about our research project this term. In groups of four we had to find four facts from the internet about a bird native to Australia. Then we had to find ways to check the accuracy of the statements. My group chose magpies.

We worked out we'd need to take one statement each and then find a way to test if it was accurate. We agreed to let each other know anything we learned that might be relevant to proving the other statements.

The statements we selected were:

1 There are nine species of magpies indicated by their different feather patterns. (Geoff)
2 Magpies can hear the sound of grubs and worms under the ground. (Kingie)
3 Magpies are excellent mimics. (Mary Lyn)
4 Magpies are unable to recognise human faces. (Suki)

I had to work on the first statement. I decided to observe and take photos of the magpies in our garden each day for a month. I emailed several of my friends who lived interstate and asked them to take photos of the magpies in their areas as well.

When I compared the photos they sent, I found three distinctly different black and white feather patterns. While this didn't prove the statement was correct, it did confirm that the feather patterns of magpies differ in different areas.

While I was observing the magpies each day, I noticed some were imitating kookaburras. I emailed that information to Mary Lyn. They are such beautiful singers, especially when they carol together.

Before doing this project I doubt if I'd have noticed but I can now tell the magpies in the park are quite comfortable having me around. They certainly recognise me, although I don't know how. Maybe Suki will find her statement was untrue!

Love
Geoff

1 How many students were in each group?
A one B two C three D four

2 Who was researching whether magpies can recognise human faces?
A Geoff B Kingie
C Mary Lyn D Suki

3 Why does Geoff collect photos of magpies?
A to put on the cover of his project
B to show to his group
C to have a record of the feather patterns
D to send to his uncle

4 Choose **all** that apply. As well as learning about magpies, the students were learning to
A cooperate in a group.
B think for themselves.
C be ornithologists.
D realise that information on the internet could be untrustworthy or out of date.

5 How would you describe Geoff's attitude to his project?
A fairly interested
B very interested
C not very interested
D uninterested

6 Which of the statements would be most difficult to test?

....

....

Answers and explanations on page 124

SPELLING

Rewrite the misspelt words in questions 1–4.

1 My uncle is an ornotheologist.

2 Is that information relavent?

3 Did you know magpies can immitate people whistling?

4 I was not sure if they could reconise me.

5 Write three words from the word family that includes **comfortable**.

VOCABULARY

Circle the answers that have the nearest meaning to the underlined words in questions 6–7.

6 We weren't able to confirm all the evidence.

A check
B underpin
C explain
D settle

7 Not all I learned was relevant to our research questions.

A significant
B apt
C related
D appropriate

8 Add a word from the text to the sentence.

I live in Victoria but some of my friends live ....

9 Write a word from the text to match the meaning.

to look at carefully in order to see or learn something

Circle the word that does **not** belong.

10 A correct
B false
C accurate
D reliable

11 A imitate
B mimic
C copy
D rehearse

GRAMMAR

12 Circle the noun group that includes an adjectival phrase.

I've made friends with the magpies in the park.

13 Add an auxiliary (helping) verb to complete the sentence.

I promised I .... send my uncle the photos I'd collected.

14 Complete the sentence with a modal adverb from the text.

They .... sing beautifully!

15 Which word connects the subordinate clause to the main clause?

I'm going to be an ornithologist if I pass my exams.

A to
B an
C ornithologist
D if

PUNCTUATION

Rewrite the sentences correctly.

16 we found three distinctly different patterns

17 before doing this i doubt if id have noticed

18 i dont know how they do it

Answers and explanations on page 124

TEXTS IN CONTEXT

Text 2

How to become a birdwatcher

Birdwatching is a popular hobby. You can see birds almost anywhere you go in Australia and there are around 800 different bird species to look for.

1 Get or borrow some binoculars. It is best for them to be waterproof and to have magnification of 8 x 32 or 10 x 42. Remember to bring binoculars to the eyes, not vice versa, so you see the bird immediately.

2 Learn what you can about Australian birds in your area so you know what to look for. Get up early as around dawn is the best time to see and listen to birds.

3 Go for walks and notice the size, shape, colour and markings of the birds you see and listen to their birdcalls.

4 Make a record of your sightings.

1 Text 2 is
- **A** a recount.
- **B** an explanation.
- **C** a procedure.
- **D** a response.

2 The purpose of Text 1 in Unit 22A is to
- **A** retell how a research project was carried out.
- **B** describe magpies and their habits.
- **C** persuade Uncle Bill to assist in the research project.
- **D** analyse a research project.

3 The numbered lists in Text 1 (Unit 22A) and Text 2
- **A** both follow a time sequence.
- **B** both outline steps to follow.
- **C** are both about how to observe magpies.
- **D** are different kinds of lists.

4 The author of Text 2 aims to
- **A** make birdwatching sound inviting.
- **B** show off about how well informed they are.
- **C** share their enthusiasm for birdwatching.
- **D** offer practical advice about birdwatching.

5 Choose the best answer. Text 1 in Unit 22A is more .... than Text 2.
- **A** dramatic
- **B** personal
- **C** useful
- **D** biased

6 Does birdwatching appeal to you as a hobby? Why or why not?

....

....

....

....

7 Search the internet for two or three recordings of magpies singing. Write down the name of your favourite website.

Answers and explanations on page 124

 Text 1

Step into the future

Ms O'Sullivan: So Year 5, the question is: Will our world in the year 2050 be very different or much the same?

Skye: That's just 30 years away. Not too different perhaps?

Dora: Society has changed a lot already though. It's become more multicultural, robots have been improved, social media has expanded. And now those changes have happened, the next steps definitely will happen more quickly.

Lee: True. And look at changes in our daily lives over the last three decades. Phones have shrunk. Computers have streamlined. I think you'll hardly recognise the daily life you know now. Cars could drive themselves, for example.

Skye: Yes, these are improvements but it's not as if we are going to find ourselves living on Mars.

Billy: Dad says prices have doubled and when we are parents we won't be able to afford a separate house. Where will we live? Maybe there'll be disposable houses we share. We could have robots to care for us!

Dora: Maybe. I think technological changes will bring about an extremely different world in almost no time at all. You can see it already in schools. On Grandparents Day, Gran was astonished at how we are using technology for learning in the classroom. The next step could be no classrooms at all.

Lee: Sure thing. And the changes are happening at a faster rate all the time, as you suggested earlier. My guess is we can't imagine today how different life will be in 2050.

Ms O'Sullivan: Well done Year 5. Let's look at some sites about the topic I've collected for you. Then we can come back to the question tomorrow. Some of you may change your mind!

1 Who suggests the world may not be too different in 2050?
A Skye B Dora C Lee D Billy

2 Whose dad says prices have doubled?
A Skye B Dora C Lee D Billy

3 Dora's gran was astonished by their classroom because
A she'd never been in a classroom.
B technologies were rarely used in her own classroom.
C she wanted to show Dora she liked her school.
D she thought it prevented children from learning.

4 Ms O'Sullivan wants her students to see sites on the topic because she
A is disappointed with their comments.
B wants them to learn how to listen.
C wants them to consider what others have to say.
D wants them to see how well they did.

5 Who argues the most convincingly?
A Skye B Dora C Lee D Billy

6 Is it possible that the 'next step could be no classrooms at all' (lines 17–18)?

Answers and explanations on pages 124–125

SPELLING

Rewrite the misspelt words in questions 1–4.

1 We live in a multieculturell society.

2 I'd love to live in a disposeable house!

3 Tecknological change happens very quickly.

4 Many improvments have been made.

5 Write three words from the word family that includes **change**.

VOCABULARY

Circle the answers that have the nearest meaning to the underlined words in questions 6–7.

6 The future is sure to make changes in our lives.

A transitions
B amendments
C differences
D revisions

7 Do you think robots will bring improvements to society?

A changes
B advances
C recovery
D corrections

8 Add a word from the text to the sentence.

The classroom of today is ______ from the classroom of yesterday.

9 Write a word from the text to match the meaning.

designed for or capable of being thrown away after being used or used up

Circle the word that does **not** belong.

10 A subject
B topic
C issue
D fact

11 A guess
B calculation
C assumption
D hunch

GRAMMAR

12 Circle the noun group that includes an adjectival phrase.

The teacher showed us some sites about the topic.

13 Add an auxiliary (helping) verb to complete the sentence.

______ you imagine what it will be like?

14 Complete the sentence with a modal adverb from the text.

Since then change has ______ happened more quickly.

15 Which word connects the subordinate clause to the main clause?

We looked at the websites after the bell rang for class.

A at
B websites
C after
D the

PUNCTUATION

Rewrite the sentences correctly.

16 thats hardly any time to wait

17 they went to doras classroom on grandparents day

18 perhaps its not too different

Answers and explanations on page 125

TEXTS IN CONTEXT

Text 2

What's new?

The **Help-u-out Robot** is new. What can it do? Well, let's say you need a pet but can't have one in your city unit—**Help-u-out** will come to your rescue. It can follow you around, keep you company and even dance with you if you're in the mood. It can carry things to you when you need them and turn lights and TVs on or off at your command. Ask it a question and it will tell you the answer.

What else is new? The low, low price. Visit Help-u-out Electronics today to see what we can do for **your** tomorrow.

1 The main purpose of Text 2 is to .... the Help-u-out Robot.
- **A** introduce you to
- **B** persuade you to learn about
- **C** encourage you to buy
- **D** discuss the virtues of

2 Text 1 in Unit 23A is
- **A** an information report.
- **B** an explanation.
- **C** a recount.
- **D** a discussion.

3 Text 1 in Unit 23A and Text 2 are
- **A** about the same subject.
- **B** about different, unrelated subjects.
- **C** about different, related subjects.
- **D** about similar subjects.

4 Why is bolding used in Text 2?
- **A** to exaggerate
- **B** to emphasise
- **C** to add humour
- **D** to convey seriousness

5 In Text 2 the word 'Robot' is omitted from the name (line 4) to
- **A** make the robot sound more like a person.
- **B** make the robot seem less important.
- **C** emphasise the robot's mechanical nature.
- **D** draw attention to the way its name is spelt.

6 How well does the picture for Text 1 in Unit 23A relate to its title?

....

....

....

....

....

....

Get creative

7 **a** How would you answer Ms O'Sullivan's question?

or

b Design a robot you would like to own. Give it a name and list what it can do.

Answers and explanations on page 125

 Text 1

The Wara Art Festival

❶ Good morning everyone. My name is Alisa. I was asked to give a talk about arts or crafts from a different culture. I chose the Japanese culture and I asked my schoolfriend Kaito if he knew about any arts or crafts that are different from things we do here in Australia.

❷ At first he couldn't think of anything but then he suddenly remembered the Wara Art Festival. Kaito used to live in a rural area in the north of Honshu, the largest island of Japan, near where the Festival is held.

❸ Where he lived, there are many rice paddies (small, level flooded fields used to grow rice) which produce a rich harvest each year. After the grain is extracted, there is lots of rice straw or 'wara' left over. He told me the Japanese are good at avoiding waste so they use it for roofing, for feeding livestock and as fertiliser. The university students from the area also use it to make giant-sized sculptures of animals that are then dotted around the fields at the festival.

❹ When I used the internet to find out more about this, I learned that the students attach the straw to wooden frames and bind it together with wire and other materials. I also learned that in 2017 they decided to make the sculptures twice as big as usual. I found lots of images of the straw animals online. My favourites were a magnificent scary gorilla and a gigantic rhinoceros.

❺ One of the pictures I saw showed people taking photos of themselves sitting inside the mouth of a dinosaur! No wonder the festival is popular.

 Text 2

How to make potpourri

You will need:

- different types of scented flowers
- paper (old newspaper works well)
- scissors
- a bowl
- heavy books
- gift wrap (optional).

Steps:

1 Collect the flowers you want to use and remove the stems.
2 Find somewhere that is safe to build your tower of books. Put down your first book.
3 Put a sheet of paper on top of the book and place a selection of your flowers on it without them touching each other. Place another layer of paper on top. The paper will be ready to absorb the oil from the flowers once it is weighted down.
4 Add a book on top of the paper. Repeat step 3 until you've used up all of your flowers.
5 Leave for six weeks.
6 Undo your book tower and pull the petals off the dried flowers and mix in a bowl.

Mmmmm. Smells delicious! Now you can wrap it up and give it to someone as a present. Or you could keep it for yourself.

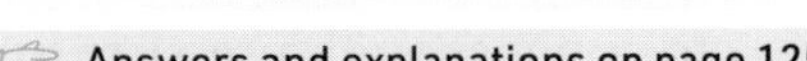
Answers and explanations on page 125

Text 3

There's a frog in our bathroom

There's a frog in our bathroom, dear Mumma, dear Mumma,
There's a frog in our bathroom. What shall we do?
There can't be dear Sonny, dear Sonny, dear Sonny,
There can't be, dear Sonny. It's one of your tricks.
Come and see it dear Mumma, dear Mumma, dear Mumma
Come and see for yourself. A scared little frog!
Oh! There's a frog in our bathroom, dear Sonny, dear Sonny,
There's a frog in our bathroom, dear Sonny, a frog!

1 In Text 1 where does Kaito live?
- A in the north of Japan
- B in Australia
- C in Honshu
- D in a rural area of Japan

2 In Text 1 the information in brackets (line 8)
- A defines what rice paddies are.
- B describes what rice paddies look like.
- C summarises what is done with rice paddies.
- D explains why rice paddies are used.

3 Paragraph 4 in Text 1 is mainly about
- A what is produced by the harvest.
- B where the festival is held.
- C how the sculptures are made and what they look like.
- D how Kaito helped Alisa to find out about the Festival.

4 In Text 1 the sculptures can be described as .... interactive.
- A extremely
- B very highly
- C highly
- D somewhat

5 The purpose of Text 2 is to
- A explain why you need to do something.
- B persuade people to do something.
- C tell how to do something.
- D explain a process.

6 In Text 2 the books need to be heavy
- A so they can be moved easily.
- B to apply enough pressure to the flowers.
- C because they contain more information.
- D because they make the tower taller.

7 Choose **all** that apply. In Text 2 gift wrap is labelled 'optional' (line 4) because
- A you might already have some.
- B you can get it at an op shop.
- C you won't need it if you keep the potpourri.
- D you could give it away unwrapped.

8 In Text 2 what does 'place a selection' (line 8) mean in this context?
- A put some
- B put all
- C put most
- D put the type you like

9 Why is newspaper recommended in Text 2?

10 Text 3 is most like
- A a review.
- B a song.
- C a play.
- D an interview.

11 In Text 3 Mumma thinks Sonny is playing a trick because
- A she knows there isn't a frog there.
- B there wasn't a frog there before.
- C there aren't any frogs where they live.
- D Sonny has often played tricks in the past.

12 In Text 3 how do we find out there really *is* a frog in the bathroom?

....

....

Answers and explanations on page 125

Each sentence in questions 1–6 has one word that is incorrect. Write the correct spelling of each word in the boxes below.

1 Dad lost the garrantee for his new watch.

2 When I had a bad cough I was given some soothing medecine.

3 I had to do a group and an individewel performance at the concert.

4 Aborriginal people have their own Welcome to Country ceremony.

5 The campaign to make people aware of waist is a big success.

6 I didn't find that advertisment very persuasive.

7 Which word best matches the meaning of the underlined word?

Did you volunteer to help at the fete?

A submit
B offer
C propose
D enlist

8 Which words are used as an adjectival phrase in this sentence?

Did you read that book this morning about the life cycle of frogs?

A Did you read
B that book
C this morning
D about the life cycle of frogs

9 In which **two** sentences is **step** used as a noun?

A Step right up ladies and gentlemen!
B Watch the step, Gran.
C Billy took his first step yesterday.
D If you'll step this way, I'll show you your room.

10 Which word completes the sentence with the correct contraction?

We .... have been able to come on that date.

A wouldnt
B woul'dnt
C wouldn't
D would'nt

11 Which verb group correctly completes the sentence?

We .... there many times before.

A are going
B were gone
C has been
D have been

12 Which word group describes **where** the possum sped?

The possum quickly sped to the roof with her baby in her pouch.

13 Which sentence shows the least certainty?

A You must not go.
B I'd rather you didn't go.
C You may decide not to go.
D Please don't go.

14 Which word joins the two clauses.

I took Bennie to the vet because he had a sore paw.

15 Which word correctly completes this sentence?

Suri, ... mother is Mum's sister, is coming for a sleepover tomorrow.

A her
B who's
C whose
D which

16 Which sentence is punctuated correctly?

A Mary said, 'I don't have any homework tonight.
B Mary said 'I don't have any homework tonight.'
C 'Mary said, I don't have any homework tonight.'
D Mary said, 'I don't have any homework tonight.'

Answers and explanations on pages 125–126

READING AND COMPREHENSION

Text 1

Slang

Slang is made up of words that come and go without anyone really being sure why. These rather colourful words and phrases are more commonly found in speech than in writing. They tend to become popular with particular groups of people and then shift into wider usage. Examples of slang terms of this kind include the word 'fuzz' meaning police, 'grub' meaning food or 'freaking out' meaning feeling scared.

Slang words are often in fashion one minute and out of fashion the next. In the 1970s to 'dig' something meant you got it, you understood it. Or if you thought someone's behaviour was boring and out of touch you said they were 'square'. No-one really uses either of those expressions these days. Rhyming slang ('loaf of bread' for head, 'Scooby Doo' for clue) was very popular with certain groups in the past but many young people today don't recognise or use these expressions.

Teenagers usually have their own special words to show they approve or disapprove of something. In the 1980s, for example, the word 'wicked' was used by this group to mean excellent or great, though it soon went out of fashion. Current favourites include 'fam' for closest friends; 'squad' for a friend group; 'GOAT', an acronym for greatest of all time; and 'Gucci' for something good or cool.

How you use a word may show which generation you are from. Take the word 'busted' meaning broken. In your grandparents' generation it was used as slang for being caught out doing something wrong. Today it is slang for something that is ugly. We can't really predict what it will mean tomorrow!

1 Slang words
- A never change.
- B move in and out of fashion.
- C are not found in speech.
- D are not found in writing.

2 The slang word 'fam' means
- A family members.
- B closest friends.
- C family and closest friends.
- D friends.

3 Why is slang common in speech?
- A Speech is always formal.
- B Speech is never formal.
- C Speech is often informal.
- D Speech is always informal.

4 Which idea is **not** expressed in the text?
- A Slang words should never be used.
- B Slang words change over time.
- C Teenagers tend to have their 'own' slang.
- D Some slang words go out of fashion.

5 What does 'tomorrow' (line 22) mean?
- A the day after today
- B on the next day
- C in the future
- D sooner

6 Why do you think people use slang?

Answers and explanations on page 126

SPELLING

Rewrite the misspelt words in questions 1–4.

1 Mum frieked out when she saw the hairy spider. ....

2 It is not only the younger genneration who use slang. ....

3 Ryming slang has gone out of fashion.

....

4 It's hard to predickt what will happen.

....

5 Write three words from the word family that includes **speech**.

....

VOCABULARY

Circle the answers that have the nearest meaning to the underlined words in questions 6–7.

6 Dad disapproves of my saying 'awesome' all the time.
A rejects B vetoes
C dislikes D dismisses

7 Certain groups, such as teenagers, often use that slang word.
A definite B particular
C most D many

8 Add a word from the text to the sentence.

Rhyming slang was more .... in the past than it is now.

9 Write a word from the text to match the meaning.

an abbreviation formed from the initial letters of other words and pronounced as a word ....

Circle the word that does **not** belong.

10 A fashionable B new
C present-day D acceptable

11 A saying B definition
C remark D phrase

GRAMMAR

12 Put brackets around the adjectival clause in this sentence.

Sland that includes colourful language is popular with teenagers.

13 Complete the sentence with the correct verb.

Teenagers .... their own special slang words.
A had B are having
C have D have had

14 Add brackets to the adverbial clause and circle the verb it modifies.

I use slang much more when I'm with my friends.

15 Which causal connective links the subordinate clause to the main clause?

No-one uses those words because they have gone out of fashion.

....

PUNCTUATION

Rewrite the sentences correctly.

16 scooby doo means you havent a clue

....

....

17 in the 1970s square was a popular slang term

....

....

18 I think its called rhyming slang

....

....

Answers and explanations on page 126

TEXTS IN CONTEXT

Text 2

Catch up

Tim: Hi Mark. What's up? Pause. That sounds cool. What's on? Pause. Awesome! Who'll be there? Pause. Just the squad then? Cool. Pause. Sure, I'll be there. Hundo P. Catch you later, bruh.

1 Text 2 is
- A a transcript of a conversation.
- B a transcript of one side of a telephone conversation.
- C a report about slang.
- D a diary entry containing slang.

2 The purpose of Text 1 in Unit 24A is to
- A promote the idea of using slang.
- B explain the meaning of slang words.
- C discuss the purpose of slang.
- D provide information about slang.

3 Text 1 (Unit 24A) and Text 2 both
- A discuss slang.
- B include examples of slang.
- C are designed to amuse people.
- D have the same subject.

4 The author's attitude to the use of slang in Text 1 (Unit 24A) is
- A highly critical.
- B disapproving.
- C accepting.
- D approving.

5 Tim uses slang to
- A communicate easily with his friend.
- B show off to his friend.
- C make his friend uncomfortable.
- D make his friend laugh.

6 When talking on the telephone would you use any of the slang words in Text 2? Why or why not?

....

....

....

....

....

....

....

....

....

....

Get creative

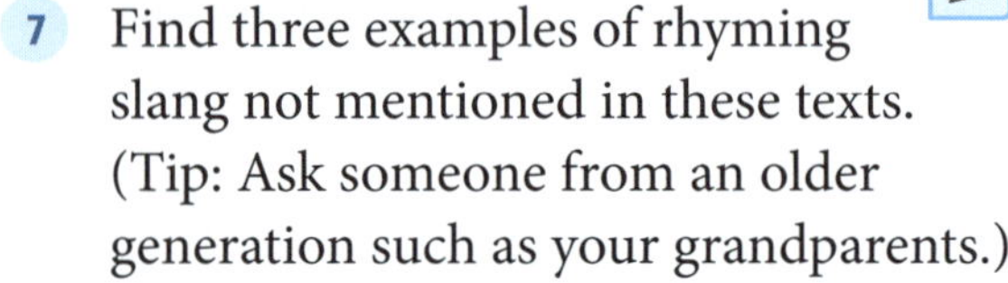

7 Find three examples of rhyming slang not mentioned in these texts. (Tip: Ask someone from an older generation such as your grandparents.)

Answers and explanations on page 126

READING AND COMPREHENSION

 Text 1

The schoolroom

Scene 2 *(Row of schoolgirls enter from left. They stand to attention as Mr Bee enters from right.)*

Narrator Jane goes to Rosewood but there, indeed,
things are as bad as with Aunt Weed.
Who's this with the Head? If it isn't Mr Bee
to interrupt work and interrupt tea.
I think there's something he wants to mention.
I was right. Here it comes …

Mr Bee A … ttention!
The laundress says each girl's … er … undies,
are washed quite regularly on Sundays.
That is the limit. Once a year
is plenty for the children here.
And young ladies, I'd like to know
why lunch was served two weeks ago?
Luncheon, luncheon? Whose innovation?
Do you want to cause inflation?

Girls Oh sir, we grow so faint and weak.
(Schoolgirls sway and look faint.)

Narrator But Mr Bee lets out a squeak,
and pokes at a trembling, fearful girl
who on her forehead wears a …

Mr Bee CURL! And whatismore it is red!
The barber must shave her entire head.

Girl But my hair is red and naturally curls.

Mr Bee Nature—that is not for girls.

Narrator All might have been well if only fate
had not caused Jane to drop her slate.
It smashed in pieces and drew all eyes.
A voice rang out …

Mr Bee The child who lies!
Place her upon this chair that rebel.
She looks like a child but she's the devil.

Narrator Hour after hour, Jane stands alone,
alternately stumbling and giving a moan.
But don't lose heart, take some cheer,
Jane won't be beaten by the evil here.
She has a noble moral code
and is determined to live for our next episode.

(From *Jane Fair* by Donna Gibbs)

1 Who tells the audience Jane is now at Rosewood?

A The Narrator
B Mr Bee
C Aunt Weed
D The Head

2 Who has a 'noble moral code' (line 39)?

A The Narrator
B Mr Bee
C The Head
D Jane

3 Mr Bee has .... heard of Jane before.

A never
B definitely
C probably not
D possibly

4 Choose **all** that apply. We know Jane is not a 'devil' (line 34) because

A she dropped her slate.
B the girls are afraid of her.
C the narrator assures us Jane is a good girl.
D you can't trust Mr Bee's judgement.

5 Mr Bee's views on how children should be treated are

A quite reasonable.
B utterly cruel and unkind.
C quite unfair.
D sensible.

6 What makes this extract comical? Explain.

....

....

....

....

....

....

Answers and explanations on page 126

SPELLING

Rewrite the misspelt words in questions 1–4.

1 Please don't interupt me again!

2 Our school is famous for its inovashions.

3 She alternitally stumbled and moaned.

4 I've not seen the new eppisode of that serial yet.

5 Write three words from the word family that includes **rebel**.

VOCABULARY

Circle the answers that have the nearest meaning to the underlined words in questions 6–7.

6 The Head did not dare interrupt Mr Bee's lecture.

A delay | B intrude upon
C damage | D break

7 She was fearful that she'd be punished harshly.

A afraid | B terrified
C concerned | D horrified

8 Add a word from the text to the sentence.

She had red hair that curled ________.

9 Write a word from the text to match the meaning.

change back and forth between states, actions, etc.; one after the other

Circle the word that does **not** belong.

10 A trembling | B quivering
C shivering | D rocking

11 A boundary | B limit
C centre | D edge

GRAMMAR

12 Put brackets around the adjectival clause in this sentence.

Jane, who had red, curly hair, was punished by Mr Bee.

13 Complete the sentence with the correct verb.

Jane's slate ________ in pieces and drew Mr Bee's attention to her.

A smashes | B is smashing
C smash | D smashed

14 Add brackets to the adverbial clause and circle the verb it modifies.
Jane stood on the stool until she nearly fainted.

15 Which causal connective links the subordinate clause to the main clause?

Jane was punished harshly so she'd learn better manners.

PUNCTUATION

Rewrite the sentences correctly.

16 whos this with jane

17 its the child who lies

18 dont lose heart

Answers and explanations on page 126

Text 2

Extract from Jane Eyre by Charlotte Bronte

'And, ma'am,' he [Mr Brocklehurst] continued, 'the laundress tells me some of the girls have two clean tuckers in the week: it is too much; the rules limit them to one.'

...

And there is another thing which surprised me; I find, in settling accounts with the housekeeper, that a lunch, consisting of bread and cheese, has twice been served out to the girls during the past fortnight. How is this?

...

I might have escaped notice, had not my treacherous slate somehow happened to slip from my hand, and falling with an obtrusive crash, directly drawn every eye upon me; I knew it was all over now, and, as I stooped to pick up the two fragments of slate, I rallied my forces for the worst. It came.

(Extracts from Chapter 7 of *Jane Eyre* by Charlotte Bronte, 1847)

1. Text 2 is made up of
   - A quotes from Mr Brocklehurst.
   - B the words of the narrator.
   - C extracts from a novel.
   - D a collection of ideas.
2. Text 1 in Unit 25A is a
   - A long poem.
   - B scene from a play.
   - C scene from a novel.
   - D narrative.
3. Who is the speaker of the lines beginning 'I might ...' (line 7) in Text 2?
   - A Mr Brocklehurst
   - B the author
   - C a girl with red hair
   - D Jane Eyre
4. Text 1 in Unit 25A is .... of *Jane Eyre*.
   - A a send-up
   - B an imitation
   - C a tragic version
   - D a rhyming version
5. Jane is called *Jane Fair* in the title of Text 1 (Unit 25A) to show she
   - A is extremely good and virtuous.
   - B has fair hair.
   - C is related to Jane Eyre.
   - D is not related to Jane Eyre.
6. What kind of impact do the last two words of Text 2 have? Explain.

   ....

   ....

   ....

Get creative

7. Read chapter seven of *Jane Eyre*. It is available on the Project Gutenberg website (www.gutenberg.org). Would you like to read more of the novel? Why or why not?

Answers and explanations on page 127

 Text 1

Walking on eggshells

It's not the first time ancient eggs have been discovered in China. In the 1990s some schoolboys found what they thought were stones on a building site in the city of Heyuan, Guangdong Province. It turned out they were dinosaur eggs. More recently, builders dug up eggs of the long-necked sauropod, a dinosaur with a neck half the length of its body.

Now a large cache of around 300 pterosaur eggs has been unearthed by paleontologists in another area of China: the Gobi Desert. Pterosaurs were winged reptiles who lived alongside dinosaurs more than a hundred million years ago. The find includes a larger number of eggs containing pterosaur embryos than ever before.

How did they get there? The eggs with their leathery shells were most likely buried in nests on the shores of a lake. At the time the birds nested there, the landscape was quite different. Wild storms and flash floods must have washed the eggs from their nests into the water where mud covered and preserved them for millions of years. The eggs were found in different layers of sediment so the eggs can't have been washed there all at once.

Using equipment such as computed tomography (CT) scans to examine the eggs and their embryos, scientists hope to find answers to questions such as:

- Did pterosaurs bury their eggs and if so where and how was this done?
- In what order did the various parts of the embryos develop?
- Were the newborns dependent on their parents?
- How soon could the young birds fly?

A spokesperson for the research team told our reporter more evidence was needed before any firm conclusions could be drawn. 'But there's no doubt we're on the brink of new understandings about these ancient birds,' he added.

1 Who talked to the reporter?
- A the research team
- B a pterosaur
- C a spokesperson for the research team
- D schoolboys

2 The shells of pterosaur eggs were
- A long-necked.
- B watery.
- C made of mud.
- D leathery.

3 What changed over time in the area where the cache was found?
- A The landscape altered.
- B Storms washed away the eggs.
- C New equipment arrived.
- D The eggshells toughened up.

4 What made the eggs found in the Gobi Desert particularly special?
- A the number found
- B the number found that still contained embryos
- C that the mud had preserved them
- D that they were caught in flash floods

5 Choose **all** that apply. The spokesperson's approach to the research was
- A cautious.
- B pessimistic.
- C optimistic.
- D overenthusiastic.

6 Is the title a good choice for this article? Why or why not?

Answers and explanations on page 127

SPELLING

Rewrite the misspelt words in questions 1–4.

1 You'll never guess what they unerthd!

2 No-one has ever seen a pterrorsaur.

3 Many of the eggs contained embrioes.

4 Were newborns dependant on their parents?

5 Write three words from the word family that contains **includes**.

VOCABULARY

Circle the answers that have the nearest meaning to the underlined words in questions 6–7.

6 We need to know how the various parts developed.

A different B specified
C numerous D distinctive

7 The eggs were preserved for millions of years.

A defended B refrigerated
C shielded D kept safe

8 Add a word from the text to the sentence.

A ______ of around 300 eggs was discovered in China.

9 Write a word from the text to match the meaning.

scientists who study fossils

Circle the word that does **not** belong.

10 A comprehending B holding
C containing D accommodating

11 A evidence B contradiction
C confirmation D affirmation

GRAMMAR

12 Put brackets around the adjectival clause in this sentence.

The stones that were found by the boys turned out to be eggs.

13 Complete the sentence with the correct verb or verb group.

The team ______ to search for the nests yesterday.

A has gone B went
C will go D are going

14 Add brackets to the adverbial clause and circle the verb it modifies.

After we'd been digging for days we found sauropod eggs.

15 Which temporal connective links the subordinate clause to the main clause?

I'd like to be a paleontologist when I grow up.

PUNCTUATION

Rewrite the sentences correctly.

16 its not the first time

17 eggs of the sauropod a long-necked dinosaur have been found

18 but theres no doubt he added

Answers and explanations on page 127

 Text 2

Egg art

The decoration of eggs is a popular form of art in many cultures, particularly Eastern European. Usually the contents of the egg are gently blown out through tiny holes pierced at each end. The eggs are painted, dyed or patterned using various techniques or may be carved using very fine drills to create lace-like sculptures. A trend in Chinese egg art is to carve portraits on to the shells—a very delicate operation! Other decorated eggs are entirely handmade. The House of Fabergé, for example, makes its eggs from gold, enamel and other jewels.

1 Text 2 is
- **A** a discussion.
- **B** a recount.
- **C** an information report.
- **D** an explanation.

2 You would be most likely to find Text 2
- **A** in an instruction manual.
- **B** in junk mail.
- **C** on Wikipedia.
- **D** in an editorial.

3 You would be most likely to find Text 1 (Unit 26A)
- **A** in a book about birds.
- **B** in a geography textbook.
- **C** in a newspaper.
- **D** on Wikipedia.

4 The language of Text 1 in Unit 26A is .... that of Text 2.
- **A** less formal than
- **B** more formal than
- **C** less relaxed than
- **D** less personal than

5 Which statement is true?
- **A** Pterosaurs are dinosaurs.
- **B** Fabergé eggs are all made from gold.
- **C** Scientists know that pterosaurs buried their eggs.
- **D** Egg art is popular in some Eastern European cultures.

6 How important is the discovery described in Text 1 (Unit 26A)? Explain.

....

....

....

....

....

Get creative

7 Use your dictionary to find the origin of the word pterosaur.

Answers and explanations on page 127

 Text 1

The recorder

The recorder is a simple flute with seven finger holes, a thumb hole and a whistle-like mouthpiece. There are different sizes ranging from the smallest, the sopranino, at about 23 centimetres long to the contrabass at almost 2.5 metres long. The four most commonly played—the descant, treble, tenor and bass—are similar to the four main voice parts: soprano, alto, tenor and bass.

This woodwind musical instrument has a long history. The oldest surviving recorder dates from around 1400. At that time recorders were often handmade from hardwoods such as boxwood, rosewood and ebony. They were sometimes decorated with ivory or other materials. Recorders were popular during the Middle Ages and the Renaissance, and can be seen in paintings and etchings from those periods.

Henry VIII, who was England's king from 1509 to 1547, was fond of the recorder and quite often played it himself. Most people remember Henry VIII because he had six wives, two of whom he had executed! But he was also a musician and had many other accomplishments. He had a large number of recorders in his collection and took pleasure in both composing music for their use and performing with them.

In the 18th century, the recorder declined in popularity. Orchestral woodwind instruments favoured at that time were the flute, oboe and clarinet. The 20th century saw a revival of interest in the recorder partly due to a renewed interest in early music but also because people recognised it was an excellent first instrument to learn. Before long, children everywhere in homes and schools were learning the recorder. It continues to be popular today and has featured in modern compositions by groups such as the Beatles and scores for films such as that for *Lord of the Rings*.

1 To which voice part is the treble recorder similar?
   - A bass
   - B tenor
   - C soprano
   - D alto

2 Recorders
   - A are all of similar size.
   - B are all the same size.
   - C are all quite small.
   - D range from small to quite large.

3 The word wood is part of the name 'woodwind' because recorders
   - A are handmade.
   - B were originally made of wood.
   - C sound like wind blowing on wood
   - D are very heavy.

4 What do recorders, flutes, oboes and clarinets have in common?
   - A They were commonly part of orchestras in the 18th century.
   - B They appeared in many artworks during the Renaissance.
   - C They have always been popular.
   - D They have a mouthpiece.

5 Do you think the recorder is likely to fall out of favour again?

6 Were you surprised to learn that the recorder was Henry VIII's favourite instrument? Why or why not? 

Answers and explanations on pages 127–128

SPELLING

Rewrite the misspelt words in questions 1–4.

1 My recorder has a whistle-like mouthpeace.

2 This was painted during the Renaisense.

3 I hadn't realised it declined in poppularity.

4 The obo is my favourite instrument.

5 Write three words for the word family **musical**.

VOCABULARY

Circle the answers that have the nearest meaning to the underlined words in questions 6–7.

6 His rosewood recorder was decorated with ivory.

A renovated
B ornamented
C dressed up
D garnished

7 He took pleasure in composing music.

A writing
B celebrating
C popularising
D collecting

8 Add a word from the text to the sentence.

Some modern ______, such as film scores, include the recorder.

9 Write a word from the text to match the meaning.

becoming popular, active or important again

Circle the word that does **not** belong.

10 A soprano
B alto
C tenor
D recorder

11 A declined
B rejected
C lessened
D dwindled

GRAMMAR

12 Put brackets around the adjectival clause in this sentence.

The oldest recorder which was made of wood dates from about 1400.

13 Complete the sentence with the correct verb.
I ______ asleep when I was listening to the music.

A falls
B fell
C has fallen
D is falling

14 Add brackets to the adverbial clause and circle the verb it modifies.

Whether you like it or not, you must learn the recorder!

15 Which temporal connective links the subordinate clause to the main clause?

Henry VIII earned his bad reputation after he had two of his wives executed!

PUNCTUATION

Rewrite the sentences correctly.

16 it has seven finger holes a thumb hole and a mouthpiece

17 popular recorders include the descant treble tenor and bass

18 henry viii king from 1509 to 1547 composed music for the recorder

Answers and explanations on page 128

TEXTS IN CONTEXT

Text 2

As You Like It*

There was something to please everyone at the concert performed in Perry Hall in Cottesloe, Perth, on Christmas Eve. On a candlelit stage, the students from Perry Primary presented a medley of carols from across the ages. The singing was engaging and energetic, proving very popular with the audience. An outstanding solo item, a performance of Greensleeves played on the recorder by Merrillee Macourt, concluded the program and earned a well-deserved standing ovation.

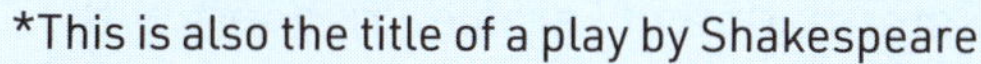

*This is also the title of a play by Shakespeare.

1 Text 2 is

- **A** an information report.
- **B** a recount.
- **C** a review.
- **D** a reflection.

2 Text 1 in Unit 27A would most likely be found in a book about

- **A** the history of music.
- **B** crafts in the Renaissance.
- **C** how to play the recorder.
- **D** Henry VIII.

3 The opening sentence of Text 2

- **A** describes a sequence of events.
- **B** introduces the subject.
- **C** describes the performances.
- **D** analyses audience responses.

4 The author of Text 2 was .... the concert.

- **A** highly critical of
- **B** lukewarm about
- **C** enthusiastic about
- **D** unenthusiastic about

5 An unsuitable title for Text 2 would be

- **A** Something for Everyone.
- **B** Christmas Eve Concert, Perry Hall.
- **C** Concert in Cottesloe.
- **D** Much Ado about Nothing.

6 Is 'As you Like It' an effective title for Text 2?

....

....

....

....

....

Get creative

7 Listen to some English Renaissance music written for the recorder (such as www.youtube.com/watch?v=N9Iv_rEKrrg). Write a sentence expressing your response to the music.

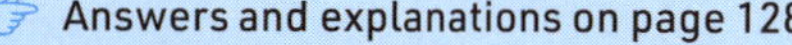

Answers and explanations on page 128

 Text 1

The Rajah Quilt

The Rajah Quilt is an Australian convict quilt. It was sewn by a group of female convicts who were transported on the *Rajah* from Britain to Van Diemen's Land (now Tasmania). They sailed on 1 April 1841 and arrived 110 days later on 19 July 1841. On board were 180 female passengers. Two of the convict women had life sentences and the rest had, on average, nine-year sentences.

The patchwork quilt was sewn together from 2815 pieces of fabric and is 325 cm wide and 337 cm long. Some of the needlewomen were experienced and others inexperienced. It was made in the pieced medallion style popular in the late 18th century. The material used was mainly cheap cotton, although some of the flowers and birds appliquéd onto the design were cut from expensive chintz.

How did this come about? It all began with the work of Elizabeth Fry (1780–1845), who was shocked by the conditions in prisons and during transportation in Victorian Britain. As a Quaker, social reformer and campaigner, Fry formed the British Ladies Society for the Reformation of Female Prisoners with the goal of helping them lead better lives.

The Society provided women and children with clean clothing, introduced them to the Bible and taught them better hygiene practices as well as skills that would make them employable when they left prison. Needlework was encouraged by providing prisoners with needles, thread and fabric.

Made by women on board the convict ship *Rajah* in 1841

There is an inscription on the back of the quilt, sewn in silken thread, which expresses gratitude to the Convict Ship Committee in Britain for caring about the women's welfare during their voyage and providing materials and equipment for them.

The quilt is now part of the National Gallery of Australia's Collection in Canberra. It has the honour of being the most frequently requested object for viewing in the Study Room at the NGA.

1 Where would you go to see the quilt now?
- **A** Britain
- **B** Van Diemen's Land
- **C** Tasmania
- **D** Canberra

2 The quilt was mainly made from
- **A** cotton.
- **B** velvet.
- **C** chintz.
- **D** flowers.

3 How did the quilt get its name?
- **A** from the convicts
- **B** from Elizabeth Fry
- **C** from the boat that the convict needlewomen sailed on
- **D** from the British Ladies Society

4 Elizabeth Fry was sometimes called the 'angel of prisons' because she
- **A** flew to people's aid.
- **B** was very religious.
- **C** was tireless in her care for others in need.
- **D** founded an important society.

5 Which of the 'gifts' prisoners received would be of most use in the colonies?
- **A** clean clothing
- **B** being introduced to each other
- **C** being taught better hygiene practices
- **D** learning new skills

6 Why is the quilt so popular with visitors to the NGA?

Answers and explanations on page 128

SPELLING

Rewrite the misspelt words in questions 1–4.

1 She was a well-known campainer.

2 The Society hoped to reform female prisioners.

3 The convict women were encuraged to improve their skills.

4 They were taught good hygiene practises.

5 Write three words from the word family that includes **gratitude**.

VOCABULARY

Circle the answers that have the nearest meaning to the underlined words in questions 6–7.

6 The chintz was much more <u>expensive</u>.

A rich B costly
C overpriced D plush

7 They expressed their <u>gratitude</u> in a message sewn on to the quilt.

A appreciation B praise
C acknowledgement D attitude

8 Add a word from the text to the sentence.

They 'wrote' an .... in thread on the back of the quilt.

9 Write a word from the text to match the meaning.

a judicial judgement or decree, especially the punishment to be inflicted on a convicted criminal ....

Circle the word or word group that does **not** belong.

10 A inexperienced B untrained
C rookie D expert

11 A uncommonly B again and again
C frequently D often

GRAMMAR

12 Put brackets around the adjectival clause in this sentence.

The medallions that were on the quilt were sewn by hand.

13 Complete the sentence with the correct verb.

The quilt .... by a group of women convicts in the 1840s.

A will be B was sewn
C is sewn D is being sewn

14 Add brackets to the adverbial clause and circle the verb it modifies.

They provided new clothes for the prisoners when they learned about their needs.

15 Which temporal connective links the subordinate clause to the main clause?

They were transported to Australia while Queen Victoria was on the throne.

PUNCTUATION

Rewrite the sentences correctly.

16 they were transported on the rajah

17 elizabeth fry 1780–1845 was shocked by prison conditions

18 is the quilt part of the ngas collection

Answers and explanations on page 128

TEXTS IN CONTEXT

Text 2

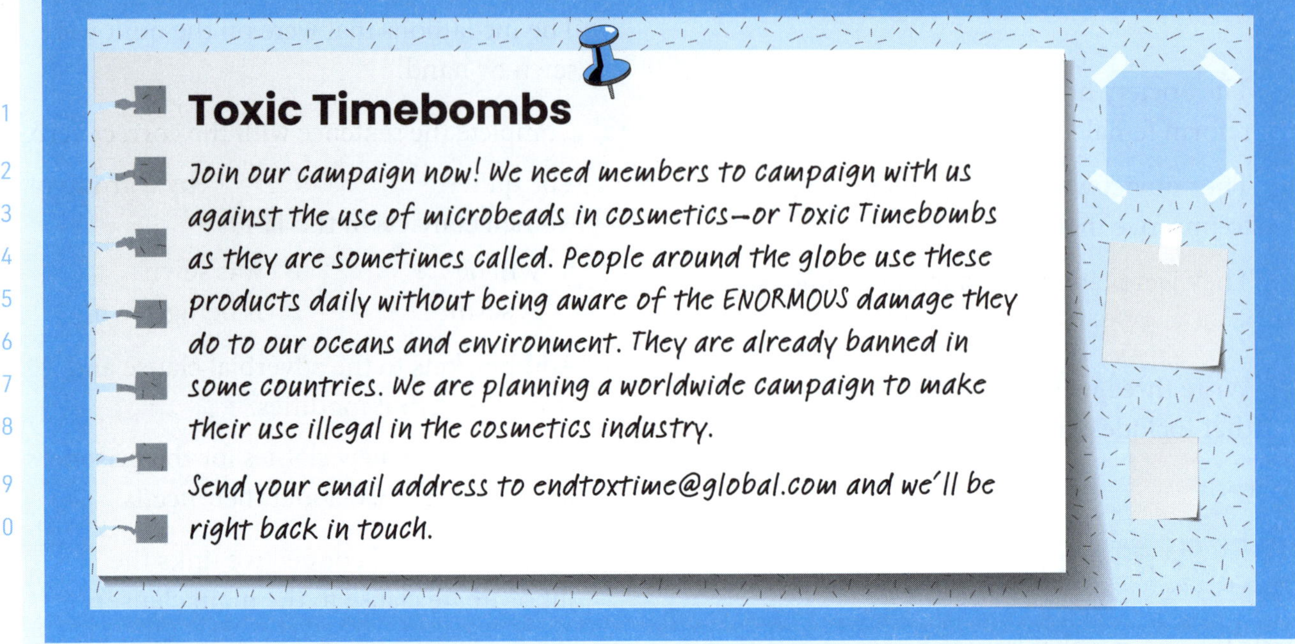

Toxic Timebombs

Join our campaign now! We need members to campaign with us against the use of microbeads in cosmetics—or Toxic Timebombs as they are sometimes called. People around the globe use these products daily without being aware of the ENORMOUS damage they do to our oceans and environment. They are already banned in some countries. We are planning a worldwide campaign to make their use illegal in the cosmetics industry.

Send your email address to endtoxtime@global.com and we'll be right back in touch.

1 The main purpose of Text 2 is to
- A dramatise a global problem.
- B educate people not to use cosmetics.
- C persuade people to join a vital campaign.
- D reflect on the harm done by microbeads.

2 The purpose of Text 1 in Unit 28A is to
- A give the history of a unique quilt.
- B describe a beautiful quilt.
- C write a biography of Elizabeth Fry.
- D describe life on the *Rajah*.

3 Text 2 is aimed at people who .... cosmetics that include microbeads.
- A sell
- B wear
- C make
- D will support the banning of

4 Why is 'ENORMOUS' capitalised?

....

....

....

5 How are the following elements ordered in Text 2? Put 1–4 in the boxes.
- A contact details ☐
- B why the campaign is important ☐
- C a call to action (command) ☐
- D the global context ☐

6 What makes the title of Text 2 effective? Explain.

....

....

....

....

Get creative

7 What do you think an app called 'Beat the Microbead' would be used for?

Answers and explanations on page 128

 Text 1

From 'The Selfish Giant'

'What are you doing here?' the Giant cried in a very gruff voice, and the children ran away.

'My own garden is my own garden,' said the Giant; 'anyone can understand that, and I will allow nobody to play in it but myself.' So he built a high wall all round it, and put up a notice-board.

TRESPASSERS WILL BE PROSECUTED.

He was a very selfish Giant.

The poor children had now nowhere to play. They tried to play on the road, but the road was very dusty and full of hard stones, and they did not like it. They used to wander round the high wall when their lessons were over and talk about the beautiful garden inside. 'How happy we were there,' they said to each other.

Then the Spring came, and all over the country there were little blossoms and little birds. Only in the garden of the Selfish Giant it was still winter. The birds did not care to sing in it as there were no children and the trees forgot to blossom.

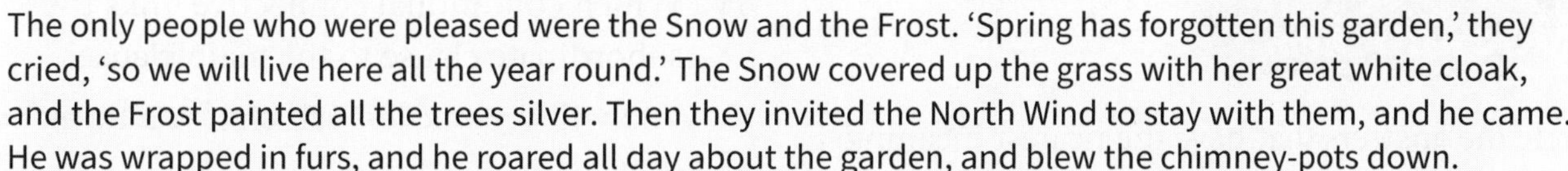

The only people who were pleased were the Snow and the Frost. 'Spring has forgotten this garden,' they cried, 'so we will live here all the year round.' The Snow covered up the grass with her great white cloak, and the Frost painted all the trees silver. Then they invited the North Wind to stay with them, and he came. He was wrapped in furs, and he roared all day about the garden, and blew the chimney-pots down.

...

'I cannot understand why the Spring is so late in coming,' said the Selfish Giant as he sat at the window and looked out at his cold white garden; 'I really hope there will be a change in the weather.'

Extract from 'The Selfish Giant' in *The Happy Prince and Other Tales* by Oscar Wilde, 1888

1 Why couldn't the children walk into the Giant's garden?

A It was surrounded by a high wall.
B The gate would not open.
C A notice blocked the entrance.
D The road was very dusty.

2 What made the children run away from the garden?

A fear of the garden
B hatred of the icy cold
C fear of the Giant's gruff voice
D the bullying of the North Wind

3 What is the Giant's 'crime'?

A He put up a sign about trespassers.
B He only ever thought of himself.
C He built a wall around his garden.
D He made his garden cold and white.

4 Why couldn't the Giant understand why Spring remained absent?

A His sight was failing.
B It was invisible.
C He was confused.
D He was blind to the harm caused by his actions.

5 The personification of Spring, Snow, Frost and the North Wind suggests

A that nature is powerful and has a mind of its own.
B the power and spitefulness of the Giant.
C what the seasons are really like.
D how the landscape always behaves.

6 How do you predict the story will end?

Answers and explanations on page 129

SPELLING

Rewrite the misspelt words in questions 1–4.

1 He pinned the message on the noticebored.

2 I liked to wonder around the garden.

3 He was rapt in a fur coat!

4 We don't know weather Spring will come this year.

5 Write three words from the word family that includes **selfish**.

VOCABULARY

Circle the answers that have the nearest meaning to the underlined words in questions 6–7.

6 Surely you <u>understand</u> my feeling that way!

A recognise B infer
C comprehend D interpet

7 'Spring has <u>forgotten</u> this garden,' they cried.

A lost B abandoned
C erased D hidden

8 Add a word from the text to the sentence.

________ are in danger of being prosecuted.

9 Write a word from the text to match the meaning.

caring only about yourself and your own interests

Circle the word that does **not** belong.

10 A bloom B glow
C flower D blossom

11 A invited B welcomed
C dissuaded D encouraged

GRAMMAR

12 Put brackets around the adjectival clause in this sentence.

The walls that surrounded the garden were high and forbidding.

13 Complete the sentence with the correct verb.

I ________ Spring once visited this garden.

A forget B will forget
C have forgotten D had forgotten

14 Add brackets to the adverbial clause and circle the verb it modifies.

Before he went to bed that night, the Giant prayed for another Spring.

15 Which conditional connective links the subordinate clause to the main clause?

You will become less selfish if you think of others.

PUNCTUATION

Rewrite the sentences correctly.

16 what are you doing here the selfish giant asked

17 trespassers will be prosecuted

18 spring has forgotten to visit this garden they said

Answers and explanations on page 129

Text 2

Looking Forward

When I am grown to man's estate
I shall be very proud and great,
And tell the other girls and boys
Not to meddle with my toys.

From *A Child's Garden of Verses*, Robert Louis Stevenson, 1885

1. What is the purpose of Text 2?
   - **A** to inform
   - **B** to entertain
   - **C** to persuade
   - **D** to explain

2. You would find Text 1 (Unit 29A) in a
   - **A** book of poetry.
   - **B** book about nature.
   - **C** collection of stories.
   - **D** history of breaking the law.

3. Text 2 makes the reader smile because
   - **A** the speaker is unaware what he says is funny.
   - **B** the rhymes are deliberately humorous.
   - **C** it uses comical words.
   - **D** it is a joke.

4. The narrator of Text 2 is
   - **A** a third-person narrator.
   - **B** a child who thinks like a grown-up.
   - **C** a grown-up.
   - **D** a child who thinks like a child.

5. The narrator of Text 1 in Unit 29A is
   - **A** a character in the story.
   - **B** a person outside of the story who can see everything.
   - **C** someone who sees things from the Giant's point of view.
   - **D** a first-person narrator.

6. Do you prefer Text 1 in Unit 29A or Text 2? Why?

   ....

   ....

   ....

   ....

   ....

   ....

Get creative

7. Write a narrative about an older person who behaves selfishly. Include a flashback or a time leap that throws light on your character's behaviour

Answers and explanations on page 129

READING AND COMPREHENSION

 Text 1

Shadow by Michael Morpurgo

Michael Morpurgo has written about 130 novels but this is the first novel of his that I have come across. I have just listened to his book, *Shadow*, being read on my tablet. It was read by two people doing the voices of the narrators—Amin and the grandfather of Matt, his friend from school. When I first heard the title of the book, I thought it might be about something scary but when I saw the cover I guessed Shadow was a dog. I loved listening to the story so much that now I plan to read the book as well.

The story wrings your heart at times and makes you feel so much for Matt, Amin and their families. Amin is an asylum seeker from Afghanistan where the Taliban destroyed his home and killed some of his family. When he gets to England, he and Matt become close friends. Unfortunately, after six years Amin and his mother are put in a detention centre and are to be returned to Afghanistan. Matt persuades his grandfather to visit them there and it is here that Amin confides the story of his past to him.

It took me into worlds that are utterly different from the places I am familiar with. It also described experiences the people in the story suffered and how they reacted to the terrible things that happened to them. The author makes you understand very clearly how painful life can be when you lose everything and seem to belong nowhere.

While there is so much sadness in the book there are also moments that are warm and funny. It shows you the importance of family, friendship and loyalty in life. I had to admire Amin and his mother for being so brave and then there's Shadow—an extraordinary dog who is at the heart of the story. Read it! You won't be disappointed.

by Simon

1 Simon has .... the novel, *Shadow*.
- A read
- B listened to a reading of
- C told his friend about
- D watched

2 Who are the two narrators?
- A Amin and Matt
- B Matt and his grandfather
- C Simon and Amin
- D Amin and Matt's grandfather

3 Matt originally thought the title referred to
- A the name of a dog.
- B sunlight and shadow.
- C something sinister.
- D the past.

4 Choose **all** that apply. Simon's reactions to the story include
- A sadness.
- B fear.
- C disgust.
- D admiration.

5 What 'worlds' would be unfamiliar to Simon?

....

....

....

....

6 Does Simon's account of *Shadow* make you keen to read or listen to it?

Answers and explanations on page 129

SPELLING

Rewrite the misspelt words in questions 1–4.

1 There were two narraters in this story.

2 Unfortuneately, they sent him away again.

3 It must have been a very strange experiance.

4 Shadow was an extrordinary dog!

5 Write three words from the word family that includes **loyalty**.

VOCABULARY

Circle the answers that have the nearest meaning to the underlined words in questions 6–7.

6 That looks scary!

A weird B frightening
C worrying D odd

7 The dog is at the heart of the story.

A middle B edge
C pulse D centre

8 Add a word from the text to the sentence.

Some .... in the book were warm and funny.

9 Write a word from the text to match the meaning.

protection granted by a state to someone who has left their home country as a political refugee

Circle the word that does **not** belong.

10 A reacted B returned
C behaved D responded

11 A detention B custody
C confinement D release

GRAMMAR

12 Put brackets around the adjectival clause in this sentence.

The dog who had a very brave spirit was a hero.

13 Complete the sentence with the correct verb.

I hoped Matt's grandfather .... to help Amin.

A was being able B were able
C can be able D would be able

14 Add brackets to the adverbial clause and circle the verb it modifies.

I chose that book because I've read others by that author.

15 Which temporal connective links the subordinate clause to the main clause?

When he was living in England, Amin became close friends with Matt.

PUNCTUATION

Rewrite the sentences correctly.

16 have you read the book shadow I asked

17 unfortunately no-one understood

18 read it

Answers and explanations on page 129

Text 2

How to plan a book review

1 Name the title, author and date of the book. Add relevant background information. You might, for example, want to include brief details about the author (e.g. Michael Morpurgo, British Children's Laureate).

2 Discuss your opinion of the book's qualities. You might want to say what it's about (No spoilers please!) then analyse its qualities: the way it builds tension or its characterisation, for example. Choose things that stand out for you and describe them in ways that will help others decide whether or not they will want to read the book. This is likely to take a few paragraphs.

3 Sum up your judgement. Add your recommendation as to whether or not the book is worth reading.

1 The main purpose of Text 2 is to

- **A** retell events.
- **B** summarise a text.
- **C** tell how to do something.
- **D** argue a case.

2 The main purpose of Text 1 in 30A is to

- **A** tell thoughts and feelings about something.
- **B** persuade people to act.
- **C** record a series of events.
- **D** explain the steps of a process.

3 Simon's review (Text 1, Unit 30A) follows .... the ideas suggested in Text 2.

- **A** all of
- **B** most of
- **C** hardly any of
- **D** none of

4 How would you describe the tone of the author in Text 2?

- **A** imploring
- **B** highly insistent
- **C** ironic
- **D** firm but relaxed

5 How would you describe the tone of the author in Text 1 (Unit 30A)?

- **A** detached
- **B** over the top
- **C** warmly personal
- **D** pompous

6 How could Text 2 be changed to make it more helpful?

....

....

....

....

....

Get creative

7 Watch (or re-watch) a film that is suitable for a younger class (such as *Finding Nemo*, *Babe*, *The Lion King*, *Mary Poppins* or *Shrek*). Write a review of the film for that age group.

Answers and explanations on page 130

 **Text 1**

From *Alice in Wonderland*

So she was considering in her own mind (as well as she could, for the hot day made her feel very sleepy and stupid), whether the pleasure of making a daisy-chain would be worth the trouble of getting up and picking the daisies, when suddenly a White Rabbit with pink eyes ran close by her.

There was nothing so *very* remarkable in that; nor did Alice think it so *very* much out of the way to hear the Rabbit say to itself, 'Oh dear! Oh dear! I shall be late!' (when she thought it over afterwards, it occurred to her that she ought to have wondered at this, but at the time it all seemed quite natural); but when the Rabbit actually *took a watch out of its waistcoat-pocket*, and looked at it, and then hurried on, Alice started to her feet, for it flashed across her mind that she had never before seen a rabbit with either a waistcoat-pocket, or a watch to take out of it, and burning with curiosity, she ran across the field after it, and fortunately was just in time to see it pop down a large rabbit-hole under the hedge.

In another moment down went Alice after it, never once considering how in the world she was to get out again.

…

'Well!' thought Alice to herself, 'after such a fall as this, I shall think nothing of tumbling down stairs! How brave they'll all think me at home! Why, I wouldn't say anything about it, even if I fell off the top of the house!' (Which was very likely true.)

by Lewis Carroll, 1865

1 What was stopping Alice making a daisy-chain?

- **A** She couldn't bear the hot sun.
- **B** She couldn't see any daisies.
- **C** She couldn't decide if it was worth the effort.
- **D** She wasn't sure she liked daisy chains.

2 What does 'out of the way' (line 5) mean?

- **A** unusual
- **B** in a different place
- **C** elsewhere
- **D** in a different direction

3 Which of these sights was the most surprising to Alice?

- **A** seeing a rabbit near her
- **B** hearing the rabbit talking to itself
- **C** seeing the rabbit take a watch from its pocket
- **D** watching the rabbit hurry on to the rabbit hole

4 The words 'burning with curiosity' (line 11) suggest that Alice

- **A** was worried about the situation.
- **B** had grown hotter and hotter.
- **C** was in danger of hurting herself.
- **D** couldn't wait to find out more.

5 Who thinks it was fortunate for Alice to see where the rabbit went?

- **A** the author
- **B** the rabbit
- **C** the reader
- **D** Alice

6 The story is told by

- **A** Alice herself.
- **B** a first-person narrator who knows less than Alice.
- **C** the white rabbit.
- **D** a third-person narrator who knows more than Alice.

Answers and explanations on page 130

7 How does Alice convey what it felt like to fall down the rabbit hole?

- A by shouting and complaining during the long journey
- B by thinking it was worse than serious falls she could have at home
- C by exaggerating what it felt like to her
- D by making up a lot of nonsense

8 The narrator's comment in brackets (line 18) means

- A it would make her lose her voice.
- B it would mean the end of her.
- C she doesn't like to boast.
- D she probably won't fall off her house.

Text 2

Dear Dad

From: NoNoah@thedoghouse.com
Subject: Yuri has arrived!
To: Akito@thedoghouse.com

Dear Dad

Our puppy has arrived! You didn't expect to be in hospital when you arranged that, I know! You'll be sorry to miss all the fun but you'll be home in a few days, thank goodness. Mum is going to take him for his training sessions and Toby and I will help with his walks. We are all sharing toilet-training duties as well.

Our puppy is just 7 weeks old. His name is Yuri. I've attached a photo of him. When the people from the Guide Dogs Association arrived with him they also brought a collar, a leash, things to groom him with and a food bowl.

It's good that we spent so much time getting the house ready for him. Now we don't have to worry he'll escape through the fence or eat something dangerous such as snail baits or poison. Still, I expect he'll need us to keep a close eye on him.

We are not looking forward to giving him back after a year for more training but we know it will help someone to live a more independent life. Imagine if you couldn't see and then someone like Yuri was there to help you. It would make a huge difference. Toby and I are so glad you and Mum decided we'd be Puppy Raisers, Dad.

Lots of love
Noah

9 The main purpose of this text is to

- A retell events in sequence.
- B tell thoughts and feelings about something.
- C argue a point of view.
- D present factual information.

10 What is the tone of Noah's letter to his dad?

- A thoughtful and loving
- B cheeky and teasing
- C overexcited
- D confident and demanding

11 Which is the most important factor in making Noah's family suitable as Puppy Raisers?

- A their love of puppies
- B their willingness to share responsibility
- C their kindness
- D the number in the family

12 Would you like to be a Puppy Raiser? Why or why not?

....

....

Answers and explanations on page 130

Each sentence in questions 1–6 has one word that is incorrect. Write the correct spelling in the box.

1 Were you able to see any diffrence between the diagrams? [ ]

2 I chose it from a cattalog of complicated games. [ ]

3 It was a magniffisent man in his flying machine! [ ]

4 Are you coming on the excersion to Hyde Park Barracks? [ ]

5 I believe their going to visit Paris in the spring. [ ]

6 She is the auther of lots of adventure stories. [ ]

7 Which word best matches the meaning of the underlined word?

The doctor <u>suggested</u> I take Vitamin C for my cold.

A recommended B promised
C offered D preferred

8 Place the words from the box in the sentence below.

of	from	in	down

.... the garden some children were pumping water .... the well, some were jumping .... the steps, while others were playing a game .... marbles.

9 Choose **all** that apply. In which sentences is **fly** used as a noun?

A She brushed the fly away from the salad dressing.
B Fly away Peter, fly away Paul.
C I watched a plane fly overhead on its way to Darwin.
D Did you know the house fly tastes with its feet?

10 Which sentence needs quotation marks to enclose direct speech?

A She said she would be there at 9 am.
B I'll be there at 9 am, she said.

Which sentence contains reported (indirect) speech?

C Are you going to Strawberry Fair? I asked.
D I told her I was going to Strawberry Fair.

11 Which verb group correctly completes the sentence?

My grandad says he .... to teach me chess in a few years time.

A used to B is going
C was able D were going

12 Which pronoun correctly completes the sentence?

Tim and his sister want to do .... homework together in the library.

A their B his C her D our

13 Which sentence shows the **least** certainty?

A The pest inspector says we must get rid of the termite nest.
B The pest inspector says we probably should get rid of the termite nest.
C The pest inspector says we should get rid of the termite nest.
D The pest inspector says it might be an idea to get rid of the termite nest.

14 Which clauses are used in this sentence?

After he reached the beach, Jim took his surfboard off the roof of his car.

A main and adjectival B adverbial and main
C adjectival and adverbial D both main

15 Which word group needs an apostrophe?

The dog is wagging its tail and wiggling its ears because it knows its time for its dinner.

A its tail B its ears
C its time D its dinner

16 Which sentence is punctuated correctly?

A I said, 'Don't dare do that or you'll find yourself in a lot of trouble'
B I said, 'Don't dare do that or you'll find yourself in a lot of trouble!'
C I said 'Don't dare do that or you'll find yourself in a lot of trouble.
D I said, 'Don't dare do that or youll find yourself in a lot of trouble!'

Answers and explanations on page 130

ANSWERS

ANSWERS

Unit 1A PAGE 8

1. **C.** See line 2.
2. **B.** See line 12.
3. **D.** You can infer that the Persian is a cat because Danny tells Barney not to chase the cat when he sees it in the apple tree.
4. **C.** You can infer that Danny makes the barking sounds because that is the only way his imaginary dog could bark.
5. **A.** You can judge that Danny's Mum behaves patiently when she tells him in detail why he can't have a dog. She also becomes frustrated with Danny because he keeps finding ways to show her how much he wants a dog.
6. Responses will vary. Danny's mum's view that it would be unkind to have a dog in the family's present situation is reasonable as all the points she makes are fair and correct. Or you might judge that Danny's desire for a dog is so strong that his mum should change her mind and find ways around the problems.

Unit 1B PAGE 9

1. possible
2. despair
3. expenses
4. frightened
5. Suggested answers: possibly, possibility, possibilities, impossible
6. **B.**
7. **A.**
8. expenses
9. despair
10. **D.**
11. **A.**
12. **B.**
13. Will
14. during the day
15. that, a kennel
16. 'Why won't you let me have a dog, Mum?' asked Danny.
17. 'I've already explained, Danny,' replied Mum.
18. 'Wash your hands, Danny,' said his dad.

Unit 1C PAGE 10

1. **B.**
2. **A.**
3. **C.** In Text 1 Danny refers to the characters Ms Parkes and her Persian [cat] in an incident where he sees her cat run away. Ms Parkes and her runaway cat are also mentioned in Text 2.
4. **B.** Ms Parkes's 'Lost' notice is full of unnecessary detail about her own feelings and anxieties.
5. **C.** Ms Parkes does not describe her cat. The lost cat wouldn't be recognised if her picture was not included with her 'Lost' notice.
6. Responses will vary. The picture reinforces the idea that Danny daydreams about having a dog and rarely thinks of anything else.
7. Responses will vary. The animal should be clearly described and details of how to return it provided.

Unit 2A PAGE 11

1. **B.** See lines 4–5.
2. **A.** See lines 5–7.
3. **B.** You can infer that most of their time is spent at sea as the only time they spend on land is when laying their eggs and looking after their chicks.
4. **C.** You can infer that flying off into a world they've not seen or experienced before could be disorienting.
5. **B.** You can work out that a puffin's instinct would be to fly when thrown into the air. By throwing them pointed towards the sea, the children are heading them in the right direction.
6. Responses will vary. You can judge that they could remain lost, die of exhaustion or hunger, be attacked by animals or hit by cars.

Unit 2B PAGE 12

1. tradition
2. immediately
3. collect
4. encouraging
5. Suggested answers: organises, organisation, organiser, organised, disorganised
6. **C.**
7. **C.**
8. wing
9. tradition
10. **A.**
11. **D.**
12. **C.**
13. must/will
14. about six weeks later
15. who, a child
16. The children saved over 5000 puffins!
17. Heimaey is an island in Iceland.
18. Fortunately the *pysja* patrols save many lives.

    or

    Fortunately, the *psyja* patrols save many lives.

    The modern preference is for minimal punctuation, especially if the introductory phrase consists of just one word.

Unit 2C PAGE 13

1. **B.**
2. **C.** As Text 2 is advertising travel, it would not be suitable for educational publications. It would be found in a magazine or newspaper.
3. **B.** You would need to be an active, energetic person to be able to attempt most of the experiences listed in Text 2.
4. **D.** The announcer's tone is admiring of the children as he/she reports the news about the record number of lives they have saved.
5. **B** and **D.** Text 1 is part of a radio broadcast that aims to inform and entertain its audience. Text 2 is a written advertisement that aims to persuade people to use a particular travel company.
6. Responses will vary. Choices may relate to personal preferences. An animal lover might want to see the *pysja* patrols in action (Text 1) or the 'appealing' Icelandic horses (Text 2); a sporting enthusiast might be inspired to try ice-climbing (Text 2), and so on.
7. Responses will vary. Students might learn that Iceland is in the northern hemisphere close to the Arctic circle; that the national sport is handball; that there are no forests; or that people's last names are made from their father's or mother's first name with the addition of the Icelandic word for son or daughter.

Unit 3A PAGE 14

1. **B.** See line 12.
2. **C.** See line 9.
3. **A.** You can infer that lumpy paste would spoil the surface of the mask and prevent the layers sticking together properly.
4. **D.** You can infer that if the ribbons were not knotted into the holes there would be nothing to stop them slipping straight through.
5. **B.** You can judge that the language of the instructions explains simply and in precise detail what you need to make a mask and how to make it.
6. Responses will vary. You can judge that the author uses a matter-of-fact tone and does not convey any strong emotions about the project.

Unit 3B PAGE 15

1. smooth
2. thread
3. scissors
4. design
5. Suggested answers: blew, blows, blowing, overblown
6. **C.**
7. **A.**
8. completely
9. design
10. **A.**
11. **D.**
12. **B.**
13. will
14. At last,
15. which, Her mask
16. We used paint and/or coloured markers.
17. The next step is to blow up the balloon.
18. At long last, the mask was ready to wear!

Unit 3C PAGE 16

1. **A.**
2. **C.**
3. **B.** The language of Text 1 is not directed at a particular group of people but is suitable for anyone to follow.
4. **D.** The instructions are numbered consecutively in the order to be followed.
5. **D.** Text 1 includes personal references (you; your) and some informal language (Blow up; Pop) while the language of Text 2 is consistently formal and impersonal in tone.
6. Responses will vary. You could suggest that Text 1 doesn't need a caption as it is evident it is an example of a mask. A caption would be helpful for Text 2 as it is not evident which culture the masks represent or how they are used. (In fact, they are Venetian papier-mâché masks used in theatre.)
7. Responses will vary. Possibilities include vases, seedling pots, hanging bird shelters, bowls, sculptures and decorations.

Unit 4A PAGE 17

1. **B.** See lines 8–11.
2. **C.** See line 10.
3. **B.** You can infer that if a child needs to beg so often that it becomes second nature, then her family must be poverty stricken.
4. **A.** You can infer that a tippet is an item of clothing because the children take it off their victim along with other clothes. (See line 13.)
5. **C.** You can judge that Mary Phillips stuck to the truth and was not vengeful towards the girls.

6. Responses will vary. You can judge that being sent to Australia is not something the young Mary would have imagined; and that she had no reason to believe she'd have many children who themselves would go on to have large families.

Unit 4B — PAGE 18

1. dismissed
2. transportation
3. Whaling
4. descendants
5. Suggested answers: accepts, accepted, accepting, acceptance, acceptable
6. **A.**
7. **B.**
8. second
9. pawned
10. **D.**
11. **A.**
12. **C.**
13. could/might
14. on 3 June 1790
15. which, Norfolk Island
16. Mary Wade was born on 5 October 1777.
17. The *Surprise* is a sailing ship that took Mary to Norfolk Island.
18. When she was 11, Mary was tried in the Old Bailey, a criminal court.

Unit 4C — PAGE 19

1. **B.**
2. **C.**
3. **C.** Home pages are located on websites where they often act as introductions to what is on the site.
4. **A.** The word 'only' emphasises how select these tours are and the urgency of booking so you don't miss out.
5. **A.** The family tree is not Mary's but a representation of what a family tree might look like. The tap is not part of the actual tank stream but is a symbol of its running water.
6. Responses will vary. The advertisement employs effective techniques which make the tour sound manageable and worthwhile; reveal its educational value and interest; and appeal to a reader's desire to be part of something exclusive.
7. The full transcript of Mary Wade and Jane Whiting's trial is recorded on this site.

Unit 5A — PAGE 20

1. **C.** See line 22.
2. **A.** See lines 14–15.
3. **D.** William does not explain his cryptic comment in his letter to his grandfather.
4. **C.** You can infer that the names and nicknames give the children individual identities and make it easier to imagine them.
5. **A** and **D.** You can judge that Vaucluse House had exceptionally large grounds, which originally took up the space of a suburb, and that it stood out from other houses because of its turrets, buttresses and arches.
6. Responses will vary. You can judge that William is fond of his grandfather because he takes the time to write about things that might interest him; he looks forward to his visit; and he saves some secrets to tell him in person.

Unit 5B — PAGE 21

1. museum
2. government
3. vegetable
4. plumbing
5. Suggested answers: colony, colonise, colonises, colonisation
6. **C.**
7. **A.**
8. suburb
9. buttresses
10. **C.**
11. **C.**
12. **A.**
13. must
14. in the middle of the 19th century
15. who, lots of servants
16. William (Billy) and Margaret (Meg) are my cousins.
17. The house has turrets, arches and buttresses.
18. My grandparents' 25th grandchild has just been born!

Unit 5C — PAGE 22

1. **B.**
2. **A.**
3. **C.** The 'stigma' of his background met with disapproval while his achievements were recognised and admired.
4. **A.** You can infer that it is quite difficult for William to work out what relation his grandfather's great-grandfather is to him. He's not sure he has the right answer and uses the question marks to suggest he may have it wrong.
5. **D.** As an explorer, Wentworth was part of the historic crossing of the Blue Mountains in 1813 as indicated in this commemorative stamp.

6. State funerals were unusual for someone with Wentworth's family background; he was not popular with everyone; and his death in England also meant he was in a remote location.
7. Responses will vary. The letter should be friendly and informal. It could include information about playing games with siblings and having lots to do such as swimming, fishing, gardening and riding. Or it could complain about boredom, isolation and having to share a bedroom.

Unit 6A PAGE 23

1. **C.** See lines 4–5.
2. **B.** See the caption.
3. **B.** You can infer that golden-haired girls are usually the heroines of stories who behave well and would not steal food and intrude into someone's home.
4. **A.** You can infer that the intruder changed from someone who was wicked (the fox is the earliest example mentioned) to someone who looked virtuous, although she behaved badly (Goldilocks in the modern tale).
5. **D.** You can judge that there are many similarities but a significant change is made to the tale when the nature of the intruder is transformed. This also affects how listeners/ readers respond to the idea of whether punishment is deserved and how the story ends.
6. Responses will vary. You can judge that the intruder, a little old woman, is dishonest and behaves badly. She should be warned and reprimanded but it is unlikely she is a great danger to the community. A House of Correction would be too severe for her trespasses!

Unit 6B PAGE 24

1. version
2. fairytales
3. deserve
4. intruder
5. Suggested answers: hear, hearing, unheard, mishear, misheard
6. **B.**
7. **B.**
8. shone
9. speculated
10. **D.**
11. **B.**
12. **A.**
13. can
14. Eventually
15. who, the intruder
16. Robert Southey preferred the name Little, Small, Wee Bear.
17. Southey (1774–1843) was also famous as a poet.
18. *The Three Bears*, a fairytale, began as an oral tale.

Unit 6C PAGE 25

1. **C.**
2. **A.** Text 1 recounts the history of different versions of the story of *The Three Bears*.
3. **A.** Text 2 touches on where Southey lived when he wrote the tale and where it claims the forest was when the three bears took their walk.
4. **D.** Different versions of the tale are analysed in their relation to each other, not always in the order of the time they were written.
5. **B.** The statement is included in the advertisement as a further enticement to buy the cottage. As the story is about imaginary bears, it can't possibly be true.
6. Responses will vary. You might like to live in a place where a favourite story was first written down or find the idea of having a cinema room in your house enticing. Or you might say you dislike the story and you wouldn't want to move to Dorset in England as it's too far away.
7. Responses will vary. The new endings could change to have the intruder caught and punished; to have the intruder magically transformed; or to have the youngest bear invite the intruder to join the family for morning tea.

Unit 7A PAGE 26

1. **D.** See lines 2–3.
2. **B.** See lines 6–8.
3. **D.** You can infer that since 25 feet is just over seven and a half metres, a foot is approximately 0.3 of a metre. Kokai must be close to eight metres tall because he is one foot higher than Jokwa.
4. **B.** You can infer that Jokwa was admired for the way she saved the lives of her people during the rebellion through her superhuman repairs to heaven and earth.
5. **D.** You can judge that it is his cruel, uncaring actions in releasing the flood waters in revenge for not becoming Emperor of China that arouse anger.
6. Responses will vary. You can judge that Eiko is jealous of Hako's appointment as general of the front forces and determined to take over the position for himself. This makes it likely that there will be conflict between the two warriors. (You can read the story online to find out what actually happened.)

ANSWERS

Unit 7B — PAGE 27

1. Emperor
2. plight
3. terrestrial
4. galloping
5. Suggested answers: choose, chooses, choosing, chosen
6. **C.**
7. **A.**
8. employ
9. revolt
10. **D.**
11. **A.**
12. **B.**
13. must/will
14. long, long ago
15. who; the warrior, Kokai
16. Jokwa was the Emperor's sister.
17. 'I am the new General, Hako,' shouted Eiko.
18. He resented the Empress's choice.

Unit 7C — PAGE 28

1. **D.**
2. **B.**
3. **A** and **C.** The writer of Text 1 has created a fantasy world of mythical figures.
4. **B.** The writer condemns his behaviour as inhuman, jealous and ugly. The people Kokai harms are described as his helpless victims and he forces Jokwa, a good ruler, to declare war against him.
5. **A.** The writer is full of praise for Wadlow's behaviour and thinks him worthy of the statue made in his honour.
6. Wadlow uses the word 'overlook' in two senses: to not take offence and to look down upon from a great height. His pun is witty and clever.
7. Responses will vary. The visual representation should closely reflect any descriptive details given in the text.

NAPLAN-style Reading Test 1 — PAGES 29–30

1. **C.** Charlie is with his dad at his Auntie Jane's home.
2. **A.** Charlie couldn't fit all he wanted to say on the back of the postcard so he used paper as well.
3. **D.** The 'haha' and the 'high five' sound like a ritual Charlie and Sally go through when they share weak jokes.
4. **B.** Charlie realises his mention of going for a swim will make Sally jealous as she has to miss out on being there.
5. **C.** Charlie shows how fond of Sally he is by writing at such length and being warm and friendly. He's very close to her but he also enjoys himself with others.
6. **A.** Sally will be pleased to hear from Charlie and grateful for his affectionate letter. At the same time, when she is given reminders of what fun it is to have a beach holiday, she is likely to feel envious.
7. **D.** Charlie's dad knows Auntie Jane has hidden qualities beneath her strictness: the kinder side that Charlie begins to experience.
8. The image suits Charlie's message perfectly because the beach-related objects evoke the beach holiday Charlie is enjoying but the large message in the sand shows Sally is more important to him than any holiday.
9. **B.** It is an advertisement for the Bakery, a place that sells bread. An advertisement is a type of persuasive text.
10. **C.** By creating the illusion that the word 'Bakery' is in front of both the bread and its background and by using a darker colour and lively font, the store's name is made to stand out.
11. **C.** The word 'fresh' refers both to the quality of the bread and to the idea that if you eat it daily, your life will be free of problems.
12. Responses will vary. You could argue that the bread looks fresh and appetising and its associations with healthy living make it appealing. Or you might claim some of its slogans are not credible (e.g. commercially sold bread isn't made with love) which makes you doubt its other claims.

NAPLAN-style Conventions of Language Test 1 — PAGE 31

1. especially
2. immediately
3. restaurant
4. It's
5. parliament
6. guilty
7. **D.**
8. **B.**
9. **B.**
10. **C.**
11. **B.**
12. **A.**
13. **B.**
14. **C.**
15. **A.**
16. **D.**

Unit 8A PAGE 32

1. **D.** See line 24.
2. **B.** See lines 5–6.
3. **B.** You can infer that Sabrina knows she hasn't any real hope of making her mum forget when her bedtime is but adds this for fun.
4. **A.** You can infer that Sabrina must be good at using technology if she can teach her grandfather how to use the voice app on his phone.
5. **A** and **B.** You can judge from how late Sabrina is at making her resolutions and sending her thankyous that she is forgetful (**A**). She always means to behave well and be kind to others (**B**).
6. Responses will vary. You can judge it to be unlikely as Sabrina generally forgets to do things and has made so many resolutions it would be hard to keep more than a few. Or you might judge it to be likely as she is inspired by her parents.

Unit 8B PAGE 33

1. goal
2. beginning
3. practise
4. diary
5. Suggested answers: improved, improvement, improves, improving, unimproved
6. **C.**
7. **A.**
8. improve
9. immediately
10. **B.**
11. **C**
12. **A.**
13. present tense
14. by working harder
15. whom; My friend
16. 'What are your new year's resolutions?' asked Sabrina.
17. I'm pleased I'm going to visit Grandpa.
18. I've written my goals for this year already!

Unit 8C PAGE 34

1. **C.**
2. **A.**
3. **D.** The author is obviously an expert on guinea pig care and only lists things to be done that are essential for their wellbeing.
4. **B** and **D.** Text 1 is much more relaxed and informal than Text 2.
5. The advice is detailed, helpful and based on knowing a lot of things about guinea pigs and their needs.
6. Responses will vary. Sabrina would probably try hard to look after her guinea pig properly as she means well. However, as she needs to do quite a few things daily, given her track record, it's likely she would slip up quite often.
7. Responses will vary. The first word in each resolution should be a verb.

Unit 9A PAGE 35

1. **D.** See lines 5–8.
2. **C.** See the caption.
3. **B.** You can infer that Tench came on an expedition from England in 1788 to Australia and that the English had not had long to familiarise themselves with its natural history.
4. **C.** You can infer that there is little or no written natural history available for him to consult. Tench relies mainly on what he finds out or sees for himself.
5. **A.** You can judge that he thinks the beauty and variety of the natural history he observes is extraordinary.
6. Responses will vary. You can judge that Tench takes care to report accurately what he saw at the time, which gives the reader confidence in his account. A modern reader may know more than he did then but this doesn't make his account untrustworthy.

Unit 9B PAGE 36

1. natural
2. exquisite
3. species
4. circumference
5. Suggested answers: attend, attends, attending, inattention
6. **A.**
7. **A.**
8. affirm
9. naturalist
10. **C.**
11. **B.**
12. **A.**
13. past tense
14. with a single ball
15. which; The brown-bellied snake
16. We did, however, decide to travel further.
17. Did you sail on the *Sirius* from England?
18. The book's title is *A Narrative of the Expedition to Botany Bay*.

Unit 9C PAGE 37

1. **C.**
2. **B.** Tench is part of an English expedition to Australia. He sees Australia's natural world through British eyes.
3. **A.** The writer begins with the earliest known occupants of the area and moves on to explorers in order of the time they visited.

4. **C.** The information given in Text 2 is historical fact.
5. **A.** Tench takes care to justify any claim he makes. His view that baby kangaroos are the size of an English mouse is supported by his claim that he has seen several. (We now know when they are first born they are even tinier than a mouse.)
6. Answers may vary. The author of Text 1 is openly admiring of the wonder of the natural world of Australia. The author of Text 2 reports the facts of settlement with a respectful attitude but is less openly admiring and uses less emotive language.
7. Responses will vary.

Unit 10A — PAGE 38

1. **D.** See line 5.
2. **C.** See lines 6–8.
3. **A.** You can infer that it is broadcast on radio in a bulletin about a local event.
4. **C.** You can infer that the bulletin is designed to make people feel good about their lives as part of a community that cares for others, including animals.
5. **B**, **C** and **D.** You can judge that the students were doing something original (**C**) and they kept at it (**D**) even when their task became difficult because they were concerned for the duck's welfare (**B**).
6. **D.** You can judge that the newsreader tells the story with pride in the children's behaviour and is congratulatory about their achievement.

Unit 10B — PAGE 39

1. guilty
2. culprit
3. spokesperson
4. concerned
5. Suggested answers: intent, intentional, intended, intending, intention
6. **B.**
7. **C.**
8. laying
9. antibiotics
10. **D.**
11. **C.**
12. **B.**
13. Could
14. with his tractor
15. who; Daisy
16. Daisy, a duck with a missing foot, is in hospital.
17. 'Well done everyone,' she said.
18. That girl's dog is looking guilty!

Unit 10C — PAGE 40

1. **C.**
2. **A.** The affectionate name, Daisy Duck, and the idea of a duck taking off suggest the following story will be amusing.
3. **D.** Junk mail generally advertises goods and services. Text 2 provides information about a new technology that has great potential.
4. **B** and **D.** The 3D printer referred to in Text 1 does a particular job; 3D printers and their achievements are referred to in a general way in Text 2.
5. **A.** The story of Daisy getting a new foot is told with lighthearted humour, whereas in Text 2 the subject is treated seriously and its importance is emphasised.
6. Responses will vary. The example of change described in Text 2 is a powerful example of what 3D printers can do. The prediction of further changes makes it seem highly likely that 3D printers will change the world in significant ways.
7. Responses will vary. Examples include toys; parts for cars, planes, rockets and houses; food by using ingredients rather than plastics; skin for burn victims; replacement body parts by using cells to make bionic ears and heart valves.

Unit 11A — PAGE 41

1. **B.** See line 2.
2. **D.** See line 14.
3. **A.** You can infer that Namatjira's formal education lasted until he was 18 years old and was provided by the Lutheran Mission School.
4. **C.** You can infer that Namatjira's love of the landscape gave life and depth to his paintings.
5. **C.** You can judge that the influence of the European painters exhibiting their work acted as inspiration for Namatjira to follow in their footsteps.
6. Responses will vary. You can judge that after Namatjira died in 1959, the Australian Government wanted to honour his life and his work. The stamp was issued following the 1967 referendum which recognised Indigenous Australians as citizens.

Unit 11B — PAGE 42

1. cycle
2. exhibitions
3. woomera
4. characteristics
5. Suggested answers: Aboriginality, Aborigine, aboriginally, original
6. **D.**

ANSWERS

7. **A.**
8. secret
9. citizenship
10. **B.**
11. **D.**
12. **B.**
13. present tense; future tense
14. through a cycle of ceremonies
15. who; Namatjira
16. Was he born in an Aboriginal community?
17. They performed dances from Dreamtime stories.
18. In time, Namatjira became famous.

Unit 11C PAGE 43

1.. **C.**
2. **B.**
3. **B.** The first sentence of paragraph two in Text 2 could be added to Text 1 as it is about a portrait of Albert Namatjira painted during his lifetime.
4. **B.** You can work out the message of the title is that 'you', whoever you are, should stand up for your own personal values and beliefs.
5. **A.** The author reports on others' views of Namatjira's artistic style but does not give any indication of his or her own view.
6. Responses will vary. Albert Namatjira would probably be surprised and pleased that an artist of Aboriginal heritage has won the Archibald for the first time in its history; that his own great-grandson is that artist; and at how different in style and subject his great-grandson's winning painting is from his own work.
7. Responses will vary. You may like Vincent Namatjira's paintings because they are striking, powerful and unusual. Or you might think they look a little childlike.

Unit 12A PAGE 44

1. **D.** See line 2.
2. **B.** See lines 16–19.
3. **C.** You can infer that it is unusual for a young person to think of a much older person as someone to have as a really good friend.
4. **A.** You can infer that Ally understands feelings can be easily hurt by criticisms and she takes care not to hurt Adie.
5. **A**, **B** and **C.** You can judge that Adie is never in a hurry with Ally (**A**); she makes her treats to eat and tells her stories (**B**); and she doesn't tell anyone else her secrets (**C**).
6. Responses will vary. You can judge that Ally would make a good friend because she wouldn't hurt your feelings and she is imaginative and unusual. Or you might think she wouldn't suit you as she likes sitting around too much and you'd rather be doing more active things.

Unit 12B PAGE 45

1. perfect
2. hoards
3. spread
4. special
5. Suggested answers: think, thinking, thoughtful, thoughtless
6. **A.**
7. **C.**
8. feelings
9. special
10. **A.**
11. **D.**
12. **D.**
13. past tense; past tense
14. with her big black shoe
15. whom; My friend
16. Of course, she can't keep a secret.
17. Well, that's all that's in it!
18. Anyway, that's my advice.

Unit 12C PAGE 46

1. **B.**
2. **A.** The poet reflects on how he acts towards his friends and why he acts that way.
3. **B.** The narrators of Texts 1 and 2 both talk about friendship as though it is very important and deserving of thought and care.
4. **A.** The language choices and rhythms capture the speaking voice in both texts.
5. Responses will vary. You could judge that having an image of a hoe in the ground works well as it evokes the importance of what the speaker is doing when he is interrupted by his friend. Or you could argue that the poem suggests friendship is even more important than work so work shouldn't be emphasised.
6. Responses will vary. You might prefer Text 1 because it is about an unusual idea or the events described make you laugh. Or you might prefer Text 2 because you like the way the speaking voice is strong and certain or because of the natural way the poet talks about private thoughts and feelings.

7. Responses will vary. They could be about any aspect of friendship or about a particular friend.

Unit 13A PAGE 47

1. **B.** See line 6.
2. **C.** See lines 20–24.
3. **D.** You can infer that the elephants' ineffective digestive system causes them to produce a great deal of manure from the plants they eat.
4. **D.** You can infer that an elephant's trunk is immensely useful because it carries out many vitally important functions.
5. **B.** You can judge that in elephant societies the male leaves the herd in the early teenage years, whereas in human societies the male remains with the family and helps bring up the children.
6. Responses will vary. You can judge that a female will have grown up as part of a herd of females. When she becomes the oldest female in the herd, she will have lots of experience and a long memory to draw upon.

Unit 13B PAGE 48

1. extremely
2. gestation
3. communicate
4. inefficient
5. Suggested answers: sensitive, senseless, sensible, sensing, desensitise
6. **B.**
7. **A.**
8. matriarch
9. efficient
10. **C.**
11. **A.**
12. **A.**
13. present tense
14. by the mother and other close females
15. who; The matriarch
16. Elephants eat grass, leaves and other vegetation.
17. The calves, one per elephant, are born a day apart.
18. They live in savannahs, forests, deserts and marshy areas.

Unit 13C PAGE 49

1. **C.**
2. **B.**
3. **C.** The ban on poaching worked to some extent but it did not end illegal trafficking which continues to this day.
4. **A.** The exclamation mark emphasises the surprise that something that looks like a tusk is in fact a tooth and the further surprise is it is a tooth that never stops growing!
5. **B.** The language used by the author reveals the author's strong disapproval of ivory poaching and its needless destruction.
6. Responses will vary. The image shows a mass of tusks torn from elephants and ready for illegal trading. It underlines the horror and greed of ivory poaching.
7. Responses will vary. Facts could include: elephants express complex emotions including grief and love; they have the longest eyelashes in the world; and African elephants have enormous ears.

Unit 14A PAGE 50

1. **C.** See line 11.
2. **D.** See lines 4–6.
3. **B.** You can infer that the title represents the sound of a telephone ringing. After this, what Meg says to Auntie Di is recorded but not what Auntie Di replies.
4. **D.** You can infer that Meg's favourite was the sculpture of a dog, a human and a rock that made her laugh.
5. **A.** You can judge that Auntie Di answers Meg's question about where she saw a particular sand sculpture by saying she saw it at a competition in Russia.
6. Responses will vary. You can judge that it is fairly easy because Meg's replies give plenty of clues as to what Auntie Di has just said to her. It is not a foolproof process though and sometimes you have to guess.

Unit 14B PAGE 51

1. sculpture
2. realistic
3. international
4. wrinkles
5. Suggested answers: especially, specially, specialist, speciality
6. **B.**
7. **C.**
8. enchanted
9. realistic
10. **D.**
11. **A.**
12. **C.**
13. past tense; present tense
14. by train and then bus
15. which; That sand sculpture
16. I'd have loved to see the *Thumbelina* series.

ANSWERS

17. I think it's in the detail, don't you?
18. I'll google them now, Auntie Di.

Unit 14C PAGE 52

1. **A.**
2. **C, B, D, A.**
3. **B.** Only Text 2 refers to Thumbelina's rescue by the lovelorn bird.
4. **C.** The theme of Text 1 is the wonders of the art of sand sculpting and the theme of Text 2 is what happened in a particular day in someone's life.
5. **A.** Meg only has the highest praise for the sand sculptures she sees ('absolutely astonishing') and she is keen to learn more about, and see more of, them.
6. Responses will vary. You could judge that the story is told so briefly and quickly that there is no emotional connection made with characters or events. Or you could argue that feelings of pity are evoked when you are told of Thumbelina's tiny size and how vulnerable she is to the dangers awaiting her.
7. There are numerous sites to choose from, such as the International Festival of Sand Sculpture in St Petersburg, Russia, and Sand Sculpting Australia. Both regularly display images from their festivals.

Unit 15A PAGE 53

1. **A.** See lines 3–4.
2. **B.** See lines 7–9.
3. **D.** You can infer that prior to the success of advertising on the *Mickey Mouse Club*, rarely had ads been directed at children. Afterwards many new advertisers followed this lead and created a new trend.
4. **C.** You can infer that the ads encourage children to think they must buy and own more and more things. They become dependent on getting what they want.
5. **B.** You can judge that 'good' in this context means worth targeting because they produce the results the advertisers want.
6. Responses will vary. You can judge that they should be banned because they have the potential to cause harm. Or you could argue that children need to learn how to cope with advertising as it is part of modern life.

Unit 15B PAGE 54

1. Commercial
2. conscious
3. advertisements
4. stereotypes
5. Suggested answers: advertisement, advertises, advertiser, unadvertised
6. **C.**
7. **D.**
8. debate
9. mass media
10. **D.**
11. **A.**
12. **D.**
13. present tense
14. directly by advertisers.
15. which; the frisbee
16. However, television advertising was soon to increase.
17. The frisbee, hula hoop and Barbie doll were fashionable then.
18. Have you ever watched the *Mickey Mouse Club*?

Unit 15C PAGE 55

1. **D.**
2. **A.** The 'you' referred to is not specifically male or female but anyone with the ability to purchase a Groovy Smoovy Maker.
3. **B.** Text 1 is about the advertising industry in relation to children while Text 2 advertises Groovy Smoovy Makers.
4. **C.** The personal view of the author of Text 1 is not stated, although claims about the harm advertising can cause to children are reported and no contrary evidence is given.
5. **A, B, C** and **D.** The advertisement suggests that those who own a Groovy Smoovy Maker will be enviably popular (**A**); the name is repeated in a large, stand-out font to build brand awareness (**B**); the picture is not of the machine but of drinks made from healthy fruit (**C**); and the claim of the drinks taking seconds to make is an obvious exaggeration (**D**).
6. Responses will vary. You could argue that it would be difficult to enforce a ban as advertising is everywhere and it's not always clear who is targeted; that children need to grow up in the 'real' world; and that parents are responsible for teaching children values so they see through the false claims of advertising.
7. Responses will vary. The advertisement should use persuasive techniques likely to promote the product.

ANSWERS

NAPLAN-style Reading Test 2 — PAGES 56–57

1. **D.**
2. **A.**
3. **C.** You can work out that the most likely reason was to make the gladiators more visible to him. He was probably nearsighted.
4. **D.** The prefix mono, meaning single or one, is used in many words (e.g. monopoly, monoplane, monologue, monorail), which makes **D** the most likely.
5. **A.** Since Herman Snellen designed an eye chart used for eyesight testing it is clear his profession involved training in eye disorders.
6. **C**, **B**, **D**, **A**.
7. **C.** The picture is a cartoon-like stylised drawing of a boy wearing glasses. Some will recognise it as an iconic image of Harry Potter. It is more lighthearted in tone than the text itself.
8. Responses will vary. Glass is quite a heavy material and high-tech plastics would make for lighter, less easily broken or scratched lenses and frames.
9. **B.**
10. **D.** You can work out that this clue reveals the gift is small and flat. This information narrows the possibilities more than the other options.
11. **C.** Jimbo really likes his gift and shows interest in it by sharing what he has found out about it with his friend.
12. Responses will vary. Sal could say it would be a waste of time as they have so little chance of finding a four-leaf clover. Or she could say she'd enjoy the challenge because she likes Jimbo and he has aroused her interest.

NAPLAN-style Conventions of Language Test 2 — PAGE 58

1. noticeable
2. acknowledged
3. rhinoceros
4. privileged
5. thoughtlessly
6. loathe
7. **A.**
8. **A.**
9. **A**, **C** and **D.**
10. **B.**
11. **D.**
12. by his mother
13. **A** and **D.**
14. **B.**
15. **A.**
16. **C.**

Unit 16A — PAGE 59

1. **C.** See lines 2–3.
2. **A.** See lines 3–4.
3. **B.** You can infer that Oliver's understanding of language changed when he learned that the 'rules' of language change over time.
4. **A.** You can infer that the nonsensical sentences are there to provide examples of the points the author wants to make.
5. Responses will vary. You can judge that Oliver's enthusiasm for the book and the examples of the contents he describes make it sound inviting. Or you could say that, although the idea of spying catches your interest, you're not sure you want to spy on words!
6. Responses will vary. You can judge that the idea of having fun learning things through the activity of spying is what makes the book a favourite with Oliver.

Unit 16B — PAGE 60

1. intriguing
2. nonsensical
3. cement
4. deciphering
5. Suggested answers: secrets, secretly, secretive, secrete
6. **B.**
7. **A.**
8. capital
9. nonsensical
10. **D.**
11. **C.**
12. the end of the book
13. have
14. somehow
15. **B.**
16. She makes up nonsensical, amusing sentences.
17. Quotation marks are called 'cats' claws' in Hungarian.
18. In no time at all, you'll find you're an expert!

Unit 16C — PAGE 61

1. **C.**
2. **A.**
3. **C.** You can work out that Pandora misunderstood the meaning of the note because it didn't have the correct punctuation.
4. **A** and **D.** The last line is kept separate because it includes punctuation, whereas the rest of the text does not; being separate also makes it stand out from what has come before and emphasises the comedy of a story being resolved via punctuation!
5. **A.** Both texts explore how language works but from different perspectives: Text 1 by offering an opinion of a book about that subject and Text 2 by demonstrating how language affects meaning.

6. Responses will vary. It is possible to work out what something means from its context even when punctuation is omitted. On the other hand, it removes ambiguity which can be vital in some communications.
7. The word let once meant hinder or prevent; awful meant awe inspiring (literally full of awe); and terrific meant full of terror. (You might notice these words all now mean the opposite of what they once did.)

Unit 17A PAGE 62

1. **D.** See lines 8–9.
2. **B.** See lines 20–21.
3. **B.** You can infer that it was the wallaby who was on a crazy hopping spree that took him to places out of bounds for wallabies.
4. **A**. You can infer that the public, the police and the vet all took great care and did what they thought was best for the wallaby.
5. **B.** You can judge that the term 'foreigners' links back to the mention of those who've never visited Australia in line 2. The idea is that people who haven't been to Australia think it is a place where kangaroos hop in the streets.
6. Responses will vary. You can judge that the television news report had the advantage of live footage of the event; something people would be keen to witness for themselves and which is absent from radio.

Unit 17B PAGE 63

1. wallaby
2. Macquarie
3. veterinarian
4. nickname
5. Suggested answers: sight, unsighted, sightless, oversight, hindsight, insight, foresight
6. **A.** An alien is not only an extraterrestrial being (i.e. a creature from outer space); it also means someone from another country.
7. **D.**
8. transported
9. regulations
10. **C.**
11. **D.**
12. The motorists on their way to work
13. Were
14. possibly
15. **C.**
16. We live in elegant, modern cities.
17. A male swamp wallaby hopped along the Sydney Harbour Bridge!
18. My uncle, nicknamed Speed, can run very quickly.

Unit 17C PAGE 64

1. **D.**
2. **A.**
3. **D.** The newsreader is enjoying a joke about Australia's reputation.
4. **D.** The bracketed information is a joke or a guess but not a fact the author can be certain about. The comment needs to be isolated from the factual information.
5. **B.** The newsreader in Text 1 tells the story in a light, amused tone though not without showing some concern for the wallaby. The author of Text 2 reports facts in a neutral tone but does include a small humorous aside.
6. Responses will vary. Information is provided about type, appearance, habitat and habits but some areas of information such as typical height and weight or mating habits are omitted.
7. Responses will vary. The story should be reported using language and a structure typical of a news report.

Unit 18A PAGE 65

1. **C.** See line 6.
2. **B.** See lines 16–17.
3. **D**. If you had a question to ask about an Arnhem Land Tour, you would want to contact the company for more information.
4. **B** and **D.** You can infer that the author wants to make an impact with the information. The pattern of repeating a bolded question with the same first two words (**B**) and following that with an informative, interesting answer (**D**) is striking.
5. **A.**
6. Responses will vary. You can judge that the writer offers plenty of detailed examples and some evidence, such as its World Heritage status, to show Arnhem Land is different, distinctive and unique.

Unit 18B PAGE 66

1. Indigenous
2. Its
3. Heritage
4. ancient

ANSWERS

5. Suggested answers: specialise, specialist, species, especially, specialty
6. **D.**
7. **C.**
8. Heritage
9. itinerary
10. **B.**
11. **D.**
12. the bark paintings of the Yirrkala
13. Have
14. Doubtless
15. **B.**
16. Looking for somewhere different?
17. They range from rivers, estuaries and floodplains to unspoilt shores.
18. We're going to look no further! (You could also end this sentence with a full stop.)

Unit 18C PAGE 67

1. **C.**
2. **B.**
3. **B** and **C.** Text 1 devotes a large part of the text to describing the natural wonders of, and cultural experiences available in, Arnhem Land. There is no account of animal life and physical activities are not emphasised.
4. **B.** An elegant female hand, wearing a ring to show she is married, holds the soap to suggest if you want to be respectable and elegant with soft white hands you need Pears' soap.
5. **C.** Text 2 wraps wording around the visual image of a hand, making this dominant and central to its message. The smaller visual image of the scenery of Arnhem Land in Text 1 confirms aspects of the text but the message would remain powerful without that image.
6. Responses will vary. Text 1 uses a range of effective persuasive techniques such as high modality (will tick all your boxes; Doubtless, you won't want) and an informed, assured tone to build confidence. It also answers the questions it asks in a convincing way and presents information enticingly. Text 2 has the virtue of simplicity but it is aimed at a narrow audience and its general layout is overdone and unappealing.
7. Responses will vary. You could see saltwater crocodiles, buffalo, dugong, nesting turtles and waterbirds.

Unit 19A PAGE 68

1. **D.** See line 5.
2. **C.** See line 19.
3. **A.** You can infer that the value and historical interest of the vest stems from the identity of the person for whom it was made and the reason it remained unfinished.
4. **B.** You can infer that people are confident she made it but, because her name is not on it, there is no actual evidence.
5. **D.** You can judge from her actions in making items to honour her husband and in keeping his letters for a very long time that she was a devoted, admiring wife.
6. You can judge that Elizabeth Cook's life was honourable but lonely and filled with many sad events.

Unit 19B PAGE 69

1. Maritime
2. continents
3. embroidered
4. Endeavour
5. Suggested answers: famous, infamous, familiar, unfamiliar, infamy, familiarity, famed
6. **B.**
7. **A.**
8. longitude
9. sampler
10. **D.**
11. **B.**
12. Samplers of this kind
13. Would
14. probably
15. **D.**
16. James Cook (1728–99) commanded the *Endeavour*.
17. The Cooks had six children.
18. Before she died, Elizabeth destroyed her husband's letters.

Unit 19C PAGE 70

1. **B.**
2. **A.**
3. **B.** While Text 1 is a biography and Text 2 is not, the latter includes some biographical information.
4. **C.** The biography of Elizabeth Cook introduces her and her family connections, then outlines the events of her life until her death.
5. **B.** Text 2 begins with the historical context of when and for whom the Chair was made, then describes how and why it was made and concludes with a comment about its present status.
6. Responses will vary. They were both married to famous men who spent a lot of time at sea and away from home. They may have discussed staying at home versus travelling with their husbands and the difficulties of having a husband in the public eye.

ANSWERS

7. Mrs Macquarie bravely accompanied her husband on journeys of exploration; worked hard for the welfare of convict women and Aboriginal people; and helped design buildings such as The Female Orphan School.

Unit 20A PAGE 71

1. **A**. See line 15.
2. **D**. See line 9.
3. **B**. You can infer that Buck is a dog.
4. **C**. You can infer that there was a gold rush booming in the Arctic and men, hoping to make their fortune from it, needed dogs to help them travel in the unfamiliar landscape.
5. **B**. You can judge that the men need dogs that are strong and powerful with warm coats to keep out the cold. It is implied that Buck has these characteristics.
6. Responses will vary. You can judge that Buck interacts with everyone in a way that makes them admire and look up to him. He also recognises his inferiors in the dog world and behaves imperiously towards them.

Unit 20B PAGE 72

1. Arctic
2. muscles
3. imperiously
4. ignored
5. Suggested answers: humanity, humanely, inhumane, human, humanitarian
6. **B**.
7. **A**.
8. brewing
9. primitive
10. **B**.
11. **D**.
12. The dogs with strong muscles and furry coats
13. were
14. utterly
15. **B**.
16. The house was in the sun-kissed Santa Clara Valley.
17. Buck hunted with the judge's sons.
18. All creeping, crawling, flying things were under his rule! (You could also end this sentence with a full stop.)

Unit 20C PAGE 73

1. **C**.
2. **B**.
3. **D**. You can see the pattern of a statement in sentence 1 followed by further information in sentence 2 in all four dot points. Claims and scientific evidence only follow in the first two; the last two do not compare dogs with humans in the same way.
4. **B**. The narrator is outside the text looking in at events and characters and telling about them from his point of view.
5. Responses will vary. You could argue that there is no connection as the text is factual and the picture suggests dogs can read, which is pure fantasy. Or you could take the picture as an amusing comment on the text confirming that dogs really are clever!
6. Responses will vary. The title is not explicitly referred to in the extract but hovers at the back of your mind casting a shadow over life in the sun-kissed Valley. The extract suggests that the Arctic, where it is hinted Buck will be taken, is a wild, primitive place.
7. Responses will vary. Something that represents the wild should be included.

Unit 21A PAGE 74

1. **D**. See lines 5–6.
2. **A**. See lines 8–10.
3. **C** and **D**. Millie says 'Get that!' to show how surprising she thinks her audience will find her discovery that Australia also had famous suffragettes (**C**) and they earned women's suffrage for Australia before Emmeline Pankhurst and others earned it for Britain (**D**).
4. **B**. You can judge that Millie gets quite excited about what she learns and is enthusiastic about passing on her discoveries to her audience.
5. **B**. Millie delivers her speech with self-assurance without showing signs of nervousness or of sounding swollen headed.
6. Responses will vary. You can judge that, on the whole, it is an excellent speech because the speaker communicates with the audience in a warm, engaging way and structures her talk by raising interesting questions and gradually revealing their answers. Or you might want to lower her grade because she uses some expressions (Get that!) which aren't appropriate in this context.

Unit 21B PAGE 75

1. suffragette
2. Parliament
3. campaigned
4. federated
5. Suggested answers: hero, heroic, heroism, unheroic, heroically

ANSWERS

6. **C.**
7. **B.**
8. complicated
9. radical
10. **B.**
11. **A.**
12. my research into women's suffrage
13. did
14. probably
15. **A.**
16. Did I have a lot to learn!
17. Of course, there was plenty still to be done.
18. Women's suffrage was achieved slowly.

Unit 21C PAGE 76

1. **A.**
2. **C.**
3. **A**. There is no indication of the gender of any of the students but answers to the other questions can be calculated from the table.
4. **C.** The language Millie uses in her speech is often quite formal, as in paragraph 3, but she also uses some colloquial expressions (you guessed it; Get that!).
5. **D.** The information in both Texts 1 and 2 is based on research, though of different kinds.
6. 3 **B**, 4 **D**, 5 **A**, 6 **C.**
7. Responses will vary. The table in Text 2 provides a model for the way research results can be presented.

Unit 22A PAGE 77

1. **D.** See line 4.
2. **D.** See line 12.
3. **C.** You can infer that Geoff wants to compare the feather patterns of magpies from different places as this is evidence that indicates a different species.
4. **A**, **B** and **D.** You can infer that the research project gave students the chance to work together as a group as well as independently; think things out for themselves; and recognise that not all information on the internet is current and trustworthy.
5. **B.** You can judge that the amount of detail Geoff shares with his uncle about the project and his dedication to following his research through are evidence of strong interest.
6. Responses will vary. You can judge that number 4 would be the most difficult as there is no way for students to test what it is magpies respond to (colour? scent? facial features?) when they act positively towards humans.

Unit 22B PAGE 78

1. ornithologist
2. relevant
3. imitate
4. recognise
5. Suggested answers: comfort, uncomfortable, comfortably, discomfort, comforting
6. **A.**
7. **C.**
8. interstate
9. observe
10. **B.**
11. **D.**
12. the magpies in the park
13. would
14. certainly
15. **D.**
16. We found three distinctly different patterns.
17. Before doing this, I doubt if I'd have noticed.
18. I don't know how they do it!

Unit 22C PAGE 79

1. **C.**
2. **A.**
3. **D.** The items in the Text 1 list are statements about magpies while those in the Text 2 list are steps to follow when you begin to birdwatch.
4. **D.** Text 2 contains tips and practical advice about which binoculars to buy, how to use them, when to go birdwatching, etc.
5. **B.** Text 1 is a letter to a relative and it mentions class members by name, making it more personal than Text 2 which is written for a general audience.
6. Responses will vary. You might dislike the idea as you prefer more active, hands-on hobbies; you may feel you haven't the kind of patience needed; or you might be afraid of birds. On the other hand, you might love the thought of being in nature; listening to birdsong; and learning to understand more about birds.
7. Responses will vary. Suggested answers: Australian magpie singing; Three Australian magpies sing in unison (both from YouTube).

Unit 23A PAGE 80

1. **A.** See line 4.
2. **D.** See line 12.
3. **B.** You can infer that Dora's gran was of an earlier generation when classrooms made much less use of technologies for teaching and learning.
4. **C.** You can infer that Ms O'Sullivan is pleased with her students and she thinks their next step should be to broaden their understanding by considering others' opinions.

5. Responses will vary. You could, for example, judge that Dora's comments cover the widest range of changes and she supports her predictions well with examples.
6. Responses will vary. You can judge that if the rate of technological development accelerates then it is certainly possible that in the future learning will take place outside of classroom walls. There is also the recent example of remote learning during the COVID-19 pandemic. Or you could judge that it is highly unlikely classrooms will disappear as meeting face to face will always be essential.

Unit 23B PAGE 81

1. multicultural
2. disposable
3. Technological
4. improvements
5. Suggested answers: changes, changing, changeable, exchange, changed
6. C.
7. B.
8. different
9. disposable
10. D.
11. B.
12. some sites about the topic
13. Can
14. definitely
15. C.
16. That's hardly any time to wait!
17. They went to Dora's classroom on Grandparents Day.
18. Perhaps it's not too different.

Unit 23C PAGE 82

1. C.
2. D.
3. **C.** Text 1 is about predicting the future and Text 2 is about a new robot that could change the future. The subjects are different but, because robots are part of the way the future is developing, they are related.
4. **B.** The name of the product is in bold to make sure the reader's attention will be caught and drawn to the brand name. The word 'your' is bolded to emphasise how concerned the company is for its customers' wellbeing.
5. **A.** The omission of the word 'Robot' in the name turns the machine from a robot to a friendly person who wants to look after its owner.
6. Responses will vary. The title, 'Step into the future', is not something you can literally do. You can only imagine yourself there metaphorically. The image relates extremely well to this as the feet face the future but are unable to pass the line labelled 'FUTURE'.
7. Responses will vary. You could argue that things will be dramatically different because climate change is likely to cause food shortages; or that space travel will take people to live on Mars (a). The robot you design should have its own distinctive name, appearance and abilities (b).

NAPLAN-style Reading Test 3 PAGES 83–84

1. **B.** Kaito used to live in northern Japan but now he is at school in Australia.
2. **A.** The bracketed words tell you what rice paddies are.
3. **C.** Paragraph 4 is about how the straw is turned into sculptures and what they look like.
4. **D.** You are able to interact with the sculptures by climbing inside and becoming part of them but this is a fairly low level of interactivity.
5. **C.** It is a procedural text.
6. **B.** You can work out that weight is needed to press down on the flowers to help dry out the moisture.
7. **C** and **D.** The gift wrap is labelled optional because it will only be needed if you want to give a wrapped gift to someone.
8. **A.** The words refer to putting some of the flowers from your collection on the paper.
9. Newspaper would work well as it is very absorbent and the flowers need to be completely dried out.
10. **B.** It has the rhythm of a song or poem.
11. **D.** The expression 'one of your tricks' suggests that his Mumma knows it is quite common for Sonny to play tricks.
12. The word 'Oh' marks a change in the rhythm from Sonny's words in line 1. It draws attention to the fact that Mumma has now seen the frog. Now she believes him!

NAPLAN-style Conventions of Language Test 3 PAGE 85

1. guarantee
2. medicine
3. individual
4. Aboriginal
5. waste
6. advertisement
7. **B.**
8. **D.**
9. **B** and **C.**
10. **C.**
11. **D.**

12. to the roof
13. C.
14. because
15. C.
16. D.

Unit 24A PAGE 86

1. **B.** See lines 7–8.
2. **B.** See line 18.
3. **C.** You can infer that as speech is often more informal than writing then that is where slang will be more commonly found.
4. **A.** You can infer that, although it is made clear that slang is not appropriate in certain situations, it is not stated anywhere in the text that it should never be used.
5. **C.** You can judge that the meaning of 'tomorrow' is metaphorical rather than literal in this context. It refers to any time in the future.
6. Responses will vary. You can judge that it is a way of making a situation more relaxed and less formal; of showing you are part of a particular group; of excluding someone; and of being amusing.

Unit 24B PAGE 87

1. freaked
2. generation
3. Rhyming
4. predict
5. Suggested answers: speaker, speaking, speechless, spoken
6. C.
7. B.
8. common
9. acronym
10. C.
11. A.
12. that includes colourful language
13. C.
14. when I'm with my friends; use
15. **B.**
16. 'Scooby Doo' means you haven't a clue! (You could also end this sentence with a full stop.)
17. In the 1970s, 'square' was a popular slang term.
18. I think it's called rhyming slang.

Unit 24C PAGE 88

1. **B.**
2. **D.**
3. **B.** Text 1 includes some slang words as examples of points being made about the subject while in Text 2 slang is included as part of the speaker's vocabulary.
4. **C.** Except for the words 'rather colourful', the author's analysis of how slang is used in different situations is made without personal judgements.
5. **A.** You can infer that slang is a natural part of Tim and Mark's way of talking to each other. They are part of a 'squad'.
6. Responses will vary. It will depend on personal factors such as age group, friend group and whether fashions in usage have or haven't changed.
7. Suggested answers: 'dead horse' means tomato sauce; 'dog and bone' means phone; and 'Captain Cook' means a look.

Unit 25A PAGE 89

1. **A.** See line 4.
2. **D.** See lines 38–39.
3. **B.** You can infer that Mr Bee must at least have heard of Jane as he knows she has been accused of telling lies.
4. **C** and **D.** You can infer that Jane is good as the Narrator's words are far more trustworthy than Mr Bee's.
5. **B.** You can judge that Mr Bee's views are extreme and unnatural; there is no glimmer of anything fair, kind or reasonable in his words or actions.
6. Responses will vary. You can judge that the rhymes are amusing (undies/Sundays, fate/slate); the melodramatic behaviour of the characters makes you laugh; or the names of the characters echo their personalities in a witty way (Aunt Weed, Mr Bee, Jane Fair).

Unit 25B PAGE 90

1. interrupt
2. innovations
3. alternately
4. episode
5. Suggested answers: rebels, rebelled, rebelling, rebellion, rebellious
6. **B.**
7. A.
8. naturally
9. alternately
10. D.
11. C.
12. who had red, curly hair
13. D.
14. until she nearly fainted; stood
15. so
16. Who's this with Jane?
17. It's the child who lies! (You could also end this sentence with a full stop.)
18. Don't lose heart! (You could also end this sentence with a full stop.

ANSWERS

Unit 25C PAGE 91

1. **C.**
2. **B.**
3. **D.** This paragraph is written in the first person. This suggests it is said by the narrator of the novel, Jane, from *Jane Eyre*. The dropped slate in Text 1 is another clue to her identity.
4. **A.** Text 1 sends up the drama and tensions of the novel *Jane Eyre* by making it more exaggerated and melodramatic.
5. **A.** The association of fair hair with virtue is a long tradition in fairytales and literature. It is a comical way of emphasising Jane's goodness.
6. Responses will vary. The words 'It came' could not be simpler yet their impact is powerful. What has preceded them builds up tension and fear for what Jane is about to suffer. The rhythm builds to a climax and then is stilled. The reader knows the axe is about to fall!
7. Responses will vary. You may become so involved with Jane that you really want to know more about what happens to her or you might find Jane's unhappiness so vividly and disturbingly described that you don't want to read any more about it.

Unit 26A PAGE 92

1. **C.** See lines 37–38.
2. **D.** See lines 17–18.
3. **A.** You can infer that the landscape changed from lakes to desert.
4. **B.** You can infer that it was having a large number of preserved embryos available for new research that was special.
5. **A** and **C.** You can judge that the spokesperson is careful not to exaggerate what the researchers will learn from their find but is confident the discoveries they make will be important.
6. Responses will vary. The idiom of the title works cleverly to grab the reader's attention: What is this dangerous situation? you wonder. Then as the report unfolds there's an amusing twist as it turns out the words are literally true: people have been walking over the top of eggshells without knowing it for centuries!

Unit 26B PAGE 93

1. unearthed
2. pterosaur
3. embryos
4. dependent
5. Suggested answers: include, including, included, inclusion, inclusive, inclusiveness
6. **A.**
7. **D.**
8. cache
9. paleontologists
10. **A.**
11. **B.**
12. that were found by the boys
13. **B.**
14. After we'd been digging for days; found
15. when
16. It's not the first time.
17. Eggs of the sauropod, a long-necked dinosaur, have been found.
18. 'But there's no doubt,' he added.

Unit 26C PAGE 94

1. **C.**
2. **C.**
3. **C.**
4. **A.** The language of Text 1 is semi-formal and suitable for publication in a newspaper, whereas Text 2 uses formal language suited to a more academic publication.
5. **D.** Pterosaurs were not dinosaurs; not all Fabergé eggs are made from gold; scientists are unsure if pterosaurs buried their eggs; but there is no doubt that egg art is popular in some Eastern European cultures.
6. Responses will vary. Understanding our past and how animals have evolved over time is a very important part of understanding life on earth now and in the future.
7. The word pterosaur comes from the Greek words *pteron* meaning wing and *sauros* meaning lizard.

Unit 27A PAGE 95

1. **D.** See lines 5–7.
2. **D.** See lines 3–5.
3. **B.** You can infer that woodwind instruments were named at a time when they were made from wood.
4. **D.** You can infer that they must have a mouthpiece as they are all wind instruments.
5. Responses will vary. You can judge that this is possible because it has happened before. Or you could judge it unlikely since recorders are now popular with children for reasons which suggest this is unlikely to change.
6. Responses will vary. You can judge it surprising because it is unusual to see royalty playing musical instruments

or because it is unexpected in someone famous for the execution of his wives.

Unit 27B PAGE 96

1. mouthpiece
2. Renaissance
3. popularity
4. oboe
5. Suggested answers: music, musician, musically, musicology, musicianship
6. **B.**
7. **A.**
8. compositions
9. revival
10. **D.**
11. **B.**
12. which was made of wood
13. **B.**
14. whether you like it or not; must learn
15. after
16. It has seven finger holes, a thumb hole and a mouthpiece.
17. Popular recorders include the descant, treble, tenor and bass.
18. Henry VIII, king from 1509 to 1547, composed music for the recorder.

Unit 27C PAGE 97

1. **C.**
2. **A.**
3. **B.** The opening sentence introduces the reader to what the review is about: a successful concert in Perth held on Christmas Eve.
4. **C.** You can tell that the author was enthusiastic because of the warm tone of the review and the high praise given to the performers.
5. **D.** There is some fuss being made (Much ado) but it's not about nothing! Rather it's about the success of the concert. (This is the name of another play by Shakespeare but it isn't a good title for this review.)
6. The title effectively captures the main idea of the review: that the music was enjoyed by everyone.
7. Responses will vary. You might love the rhythm, sound patterns and magical atmosphere created. Or you may find the lilting sounds repetitive and irritating.

Unit 28A PAGE 98

1. **D.** See lines 22–23.
2. **A.** See line 8.
3. **C.** You can infer that the name of the quilt came from the boat, the *Rajah*, on which it was created.
4. **C.** You can infer that her care of the prisoners was well beyond what you could expect from an ordinary human being.
5. **D.** You can judge that learning skills which made them eligible for employment would give them the power to transform their lives.
6. Responses will vary. You can judge that it is a unique piece of work because of who made it and why, when and where it was made. Another reason for the quilt being popular is that patchwork continues to be a very popular activity and practitioners are very interested in the history of the craft.

Unit 28B PAGE 99

1. campaigner
2. prisoners
3. encouraged
4. practices
5. Suggested answers: grateful, gratefully, ingratitude, ungrateful, ingrate
6. **B.**
7. **A.**
8. inscription
9. sentence
10. **D.**
11. **A.**
12. that were on the quilt
13. **B.**
14. when they learned about their needs; provided
15. while
16. They were transported on the *Rajah*.
17. Elizabeth Fry (1780–1845) was shocked by prison conditions.
18. Is the quilt part of the NGA's collection?

Unit 28C PAGE 100

1. **C.**
2. **A.**
3. **D.** Text 2 aims to win the support of anyone who sees how destructive microbeads are to our environment.
4. Responses will vary. The capitalisation of 'ENORMOUS' makes the word stand out and visually demonstrates its meaning: it is bigger than everything else around it. The author(s) wants to stress the seriousness and scale of the problem.
5. **A** 4, **B** 2, **C** 1, **D** 3
6. Responses will vary. The alliteration of the title draws attention; the language choice is highly emotive; the claim that microbeads are poisonous and a disaster waiting to happen is dramatic and worrying.

7. Responses will vary. An app with this name is likely to be used to check a product to see if it contains microbeads. If it does, the buyer will know not to buy that product—they can beat the microbead that way!

Unit 29A PAGE 101

1. **A.** See line 4.
2. **C.** See line 2.
3. **B.** You can infer that the Giant's selfishness causes him to behave in ways that bring unhappiness to others.
4. **D.** You can infer that the Giant failed to connect the absence of Spring with his own selfish behaviour.
5. **A.** You can judge that turning aspects of nature into powerful people allows the author to suggest they can act in ways that teach the Giant a lesson.
6. Responses will vary. You can judge that there is likely to be a happy ending where something causes the Giant to change his ways so that Spring returns to the garden. The image of the Giant holding his hand out to help a child is a hint that the story will take a positive direction.

Unit 29B PAGE 102

1. noticeboard
2. wander
3. wrapped
4. whether
5. Suggested answers: selfless, unselfish, self, selfishness
6. **C.**
7. **B.**
8. Trespassers
9. selfish
10. **B.**
11. **C.**
12. The walls around the garden
13. **D.**
14. Before he went to bed that night; prayed
15. if
16. 'What are you doing here?' the Selfish Giant asked.
17. Trespassers will be prosecuted.
18. 'Spring has forgotten to visit this garden,' they said.

Unit 29C PAGE 103

1. **B.**
2. **C.**
3. **C.** The humour of the poem comes from the narrator not realising he sees the world through a child's eyes even when he thinks he's at his most grown-up.
4. **D.** The narrator is a child who isn't able to imagine what it's really like to be grown-up.
5. **B.** The narrator tells the story in the third person from the point of view of someone who sees and understands all that happens.
6. Responses will vary. You may prefer Text 1 for the beauty of its images and its imaginative treatment of right and wrong. Or you may prefer Text 2 for its simplicity and gentle humour.
7. Responses will vary.

Unit 30A PAGE 104

1. **B.** See line 3.
2. **D.** See lines 3–4.
3. **C.** You can infer that at first Simon thought the title referred to bad things he would find frightening.
4. **A** and **D.** You can infer that Simon is saddened by the painful experiences he learns about but he is also full of admiration for how Amin and his mother deal with what happens to them.
5. You can judge that Matt would know very little about life in Afghanistan or the world of a detention centre.
6. Responses will vary. You can judge that the book sounds deeply moving and is also about an amazing dog which makes you want to read/listen to it. Or you might think it sounds as if there aren't enough lighter, enjoyable parts so you'd rather not read it.

Unit 30B PAGE 105

1. narrators
2. Unfortunately
3. experience
4. extraordinary
5. Suggested answers: loyal, disloyal, loyalties, loyally
6. **B.**
7. **D.**
8. moments
9. asylum
10. **B.**
11. **D.**
12. who had a very brave spirit
13. **D.**
14. because I've read others by that author; chose
15. When
16. 'Have you read the book *Shadow*?' I asked.
17. Unfortunately, no-one understood.
18. Read it!

ANSWERS

Unit 30C PAGE 106

1. C
2. A
3. **B.** In his review Simon does many of the things suggested in Text 2 but he doesn't explain much about Shadow, who is very important to the story.
4. **D.** The author of Text 2 is clear and firm about what needs to be done but the low modality (You might) relaxes the tone of the instructions.
5. **C.** Simon expresses his personal opinions in a warm, enthusiastic way.
6. Responses will vary. You might think there should be more examples; more explanation of the meaning of 'qualities'; or a model of a review with arrows showing how these things can be done.
7. Responses will vary. The review should be written with a younger reader in mind. It should roughly follow the plan outlined in Text 2 but as applied to a film.

NAPLAN-style Reading Test 4 PAGES 107–108

1. **C.** She found it hard to weigh up the pleasure and pain involved.
2. **A.** At that moment it seemed almost normal to Alice to hear a rabbit speak.
3. **C.** It wasn't until the rabbit took a watch from its pocket that the oddity really struck her.
4. **D.** The phrase means that she is very keen to know more. The feeling is so strong it is as if it is burning her.
5. **D.** It is Alice who thinks it fortunate that she got there in time. Both the author and the reader can see that it might have unfortunate consequences.
6. **D.** Alice's thoughts are included but the story as a whole is told by someone who sees further than Alice.
7. **B.** The comparisons Alice makes sound dramatic, dangerous and frightening—and she explains that this is worse!
8. **B.** The narrator's comment is a humorous aside pointing out that if Alice fell off the top of the house she would probably not survive!
9. **B.** Noah is sharing his thoughts and feelings about the experience of getting their puppy as Puppy Raisers with his dad.
10. **A.** Noah is very affectionate towards his father and tells him things he thinks he would be keen to hear about.
11. **B.** Being a successful Puppy Raiser involves real dedication and teamwork, and Noah's family sound as if they are committed to sharing the responsibility.
12. You might be attracted by the idea of having a puppy to look after and willing to help out when it is going to make a big difference to someone's life. Or you might think you wouldn't be very good at looking after a puppy and your family doesn't have suitable accommodation so you'd rather not be a Puppy Raiser.

NAPLAN-style Conventions of Language Test 4 PAGE 109

1. difference
2. catalogue
3. magnificent
4. excursion
5. they're
6. author
7. A
8. In, from, down, of
9. **A** and **D.**
10. **B** and **D.**
11. **B.**
12. **A.**
13. **D.**
14. **B.**
15. **C.**
16. **B.**

NOTES

Updated in 2023 for the NSW Curriculum and Australian Curriculum Version 9.0 changes

ISBN 978 1 74125 651 2

Pascal Press
PO Box 250
Glebe NSW 2037
(02) 9198 1748
www.pascalpress.com.au

Publisher: Vivienne Joannou
Project editor: Mark Dixon
Edited and proofread by Mark Dixon
Answers checked by Dale Little
Cover and page design by Sonia Woo
Typeset by Grizzly Graphics (Leanne Richters)
Printed by Vivar Printing/Green Giant Press